GOING BEYOND A ROUND TUIT

Going Beyond A Round Tuit

8 STEPS FROM STUCK TO UNSTOPPABLE

AMY C. PRATT

GOING BEYOND A ROUND TUIT: 8 STEPS FROM STUCK TO UNSTOPPABLE

Copyright © 2025 by Amy C. Pratt
All rights reserved. No part of this publication may be reproduced, distributed, or transmitted in any form or by any means, including photocopying, recording, or other electronic or mechanical methods, without the prior written permission of the publisher, except in the case of brief quotations embodied in critical reviews and certain other noncommercial uses permitted by copyright law.

Six Dimensions Books, Cuyahoga Falls, Ohio
Cover and Interior design by: Amy C. Pratt
Library of Congress Control Number: 2025921686
Dewey Decimal Classification: 158.1 PRA (Personal improvement and self-help)

Paperback	ISBN 979-8-9935999-0-8
eBook (PDF)	ISBN 979-8-9935999-1-5
Audiobook	ISBN 979-8-9935999-2-2

Disclaimer: This book is for informational and educational purposes only. The content is not intended to be a substitute for professional medical, mental health, or psychological advice, diagnosis, or treatment. Always seek the advice of your physician, licensed mental health provider, or other qualified healthcare professional with any questions you may have regarding a medical condition, mental health concern, or wellness practice.

Never disregard professional medical or mental health advice or delay in seeking it because of something you have read in this book. If you are experiencing a mental health crisis, having thoughts of self-harm or suicide, or are in immediate danger, contact emergency services, call 988 (Suicide & Crisis Lifeline), or go to your nearest emergency room immediately.

Dedication

To my grandchildren and their parents:
 Delaney Erin, you captured my heart before you were even born, and I love you more than you know.
 Nyah Eden, you were the first to call me Amma, and you continue to captivate me and overfill my heart with gratitude.
 Adriana Rhys, your beautiful curls and sweet personality make me melt every time you hug me so tight.
 Adonis Jireh, your big blue eyes and giggling squeal that greets me washes away all the cares of the world.
 Ethan Casper, you say so much already through your expressions, and I can hardly wait for you to be old enough to join us for Amma Days.
 Tom, Brittany, Stephanie, Brandon, and Lizzie, this mom couldn't ask for better kids. You continue to make me button-bustin' proud of you!

 To my sister Laura and my incredible Tuesday night friends - Dawn, Holly, Linda, Marcia, Michele, Miriam, Patty, Sophia, and Teresa - You have encouraged me, challenged me, supported me, listened to me ramble on and on ad nauseum, put me back together again, and never once made me feel like I was too much or not enough. Thank you so very much.

 To my parents – Betty, who showed me the beauty in the world, and Charles, who showed me diligence and a servant's heart - I remain so grateful for your example, your sacrifices, and showing me the important things in life. I hope I make you proud.

Table of Contents

Introduction 1

Chapter 1: A Round Tuit 9

Chapter 2: Stages of Growth - Knowing Where You Are .. 21

Chapter 3: Begin Within - The Foundation of Self-Awareness 51

Chapter 4: Solid Footing - One Step at a Time 67

Chapter 5: Hindrances - Invisible Forces That Shape Us. 85

Chapter 6: Distractions - Attention Hijackers 107

Chapter 7: Weeds - Relational Influence That Chokes Growth 129

Chapter 8: Stones That Trip Us Up 151

Chapter 9: Habits & Rhythms for The Long Game - Planting & Sustaining 173

Chapter 10: The Power of Community - Building Your Support Network 195

Chapter 11: From Stuck to Unstoppable - Your Life That Matters 213

Appendix A: Values Master List 228

Appendix B: References 231

Appendix C: The 8 Steps 237

Appendix D: The Six Dimensions of Health & Wellness . 239

Appendix E: Doc Pratt Ministries' Origin and Mission 241

Introduction

Welcome! You are at the threshold of what I hope will be your most transformative journey yet. Whether you find yourself here because life has stalled, a dream keeps eluding you, or your heart simply aches for something more, please know this book is for you. It's as much a living conversation as a written manual - a space where spiritual depth, scientific insight, and years of lived experience meet to help you, step by incremental step, go from "stuck" to truly unstoppable.

I don't come to this work as a finished product but as a practitioner whose life is marked by the same struggles, discoveries, obstacles, and victories that shape any honest pursuit of personal and spiritual growth. My doctorate studies in social psychology, my experience as a coach, my heart for Christian ministry, and the living memory of my father - Doc Pratt - color every lesson you'll find here. My hope is not to stand above or ahead, but to walk alongside you, shining a warm light on the tools, truths, and practices that have transformed my life and the lives of those I've served.

Why This Book? Why Now?

If you're like most of us - especially in recent times - you may feel that the world urges you to be "well" without showing you how to pursue that elusive wholeness. There's a cacophony of tips, memes, and quick fixes: "Eat this, don't eat that." "Think positive." "Pray more, worry less." But for all our digital connectedness, real life often feels less like thriving and more like treading water while clutching a to-do list.

That's where The Six Dimensions of Health & Wellness come into play. This framework, honed over years of coaching, ministry, parenting, teaching, and study, acknowledges every part of what makes us tick - emotionally, mentally, physically, vocationally, socially, and financially. It grew out of a conviction that true wellness isn't a destination but a process: a faithful, daily commitment to "continual, incremental, intentional improvement". It's the same journey my dad modeled - servant-hearted, humble, ever learning, and a compassionate leader.

Yet, this isn't just a self-help book or a collection of cheerful stories. What sets this journey apart is the grounding in both faith and rigorous science. As a social psychology student, I believe transformation is not merely a matter of willpower or wishing - real change is about understanding how our environment, relationships, beliefs, and biology all work together. The gospel of "trying harder" has never fully healed anyone; wisdom, connection, grace, and evidence-based methods absolutely can.

Using This Book

Two roads diverge for travelers starting this journey, and you're free to take either - or both:

1. **Solo Study:** Move chapter by chapter, carving out quiet time to wrestle honestly with the questions and exercises. This is where deep,

personal excavation happens - a slow, steady unearthing of who you are, how you're wired, what the past has planted, and what the horizon ahead could look like.
2. **Group Engagement:** Find (or form) a circle of co-travelers - a small group, book club, support circle, or church cohort. Weekly sessions offer structure and accountability. My experience affirms this: transformation grows roots in community. Groups also lend laughter, insight, and momentum to the journey, especially when motivation flags.

Whichever path you choose, treat this book as a companion, not a taskmaster. There is no "behind" or failing. Every completed prompt, every page read, and every tear or belly laugh is part of the becoming. If you're a lover of pen and paper, keep a journal handy - your reflections will outlast the ink.

The Six Dimensions: Holistic Flourishing

Let's begin with the core framework that undergirds every chapter: The Six Dimensions of Health & Wellness. In my years supporting clients and communities - across classrooms, coaching sessions, churches, living rooms, and my doctorate study of social psychology - I've found that neglect in even one dimension eventually echoes throughout the whole system. The wholeness and wellness we crave require us to see ourselves as God sees us: wholly integrated and deeply beloved.

- **Emotional Wellness**: Knowing, naming, and tending to your inner life, harnessing emotional intelligence for resilience rather than reactivity.

- **Mental Health & Habits**: Shaping both thoughts and routines. This includes mindset, attitudes, and the science of habit formation - a cornerstone for sustained change.
- **Physical Health**: Yes, nutrition, movement, and self-care - but also listening to the body's signals as vessels of calling and energy.
- **Vocational Wellness**: Honoring your gifts, strengths, and calling. Whether paid or volunteer, career or hobby, your work matters and is a critical arena for growth.
- **Social Wellness**: The quality of your relationships, including boundaries, belonging, and support systems. As social beings, we heal and flourish in safe, loving connection.
- **Financial Wellness**: Managing money with wisdom and integrity so finances fuel, rather than frustrate, your mission and peace.

These Six Dimensions bring focus, inviting us to take inventory, celebrate progress, and gently address areas of neglect. They work best when integrated, not compartmentalized. Throughout this book, you'll encounter themes and practices that span all six, with tools for assessment and steady improvement.

The Science of Change: Social Psychology and the Path of Becoming

The pursuit of wholeness is both art and science. The art is found in the unique shape of your story; the science, in understanding why certain interventions are effective and what can sabotage our best intentions.

Social psychology studies how people think, influence, and relate to one another. At a basic level, it teaches us that:

- Our environments and relationships (family, faith, workplace, culture) profoundly shape our self-concept.
- Behavioral change relies on more than information; it requires habits, feedback, reinforcement, and support.
- Groups can inspire great courage - or reinforce old patterns - so learning to harness community power is essential.

This is why you'll find both scientific research and practical exercises in these pages. Expect references to habit science, self-determination, cognitive distortions, emotional regulation, social identity theory, and more - all filtered through a gracious, Scripture-inspired lens.

Doc Pratt's Legacy: Faith, Family, and The Relational Heartbeat

No introduction is complete without honoring the man whose legacy both inspires and anchors this book. My father, "Doc" Pratt, served as an Internal Medicine physician just over six and a half energetic decades, played as catcher for the church softball league, hosted and organized many parties, and showed up for his Sunday School class each week with new challenges and hearty encouragements. His was a life of integrity, faithfulness, and curiosity. He believed in continual learning, service, and the power of a well-timed kindness.

Doc never measured wellness in pounds or paychecks, trophies or titles (although his trophies were displayed in his den). He modeled the kind of living where purpose is found at the intersection of service, community, and continual growth. His famous "Progressive Dinners" (yes, those involved four houses, four courses, and a night of deep belly laughs) taught generations to savor life in mindful, connected increments.

It's in this spirit that Doc Pratt Ministries and the curriculum you're holding were born.

The Call to Pursuing Excellence

If there's one message my years of study and experiences in life confirm, it's this: transformation is a calling, not merely a hobby. Excellence is not about being the best in the room, but about moving forward and faithfully growing daily in the stewardship of the life, abilities, relationships, and resources God has entrusted to you.

This book, therefore, is not about quick fixes or surface change. It's about cultivating the root system - a deep, resilient pursuit of excellence - so fruit has space to flourish. You'll find yourself invited, again and again, to progress at a pace marked not by comparison but by grace.

Here are several practical ways to engage, which will thread through every chapter:

- **Journaling:** End-of-chapter prompts invite introspection and real application. Use a dedicated notebook to track your answers, emotions, and new insights.

- **Action Steps:** Each chapter ends with recommended first steps (and next steps), keeping momentum without overwhelming you.
- **Reflection and Community:** After most chapters, you'll find questions to discuss with a partner, group, or mentor. Don't skip them. Accountability is the secret engine of lasting change.

What Is "Success" Anyway?

Let's pause here, as we will many times, for an honest question: What does "success" mean to you? For centuries, societies have measured it in applause, accomplishment, affluence, or acclaim. But here - and throughout this text - success is reoriented around faithfulness, connection, and becoming who you are called to be, for God's glory and the good of others.

All of us have unfinished dreams, creative longings, or talents that stay tucked away for another day. My hope for you is not a hurried sprint but a joyful, sustained journey in which your gifts, hopes, and impact are realized - one next right step at a time.

Are You Ready?

Now is the moment to take inventory - of hopes and hurts, talents and tiredness, relationships that build and those that bruise, habits good and bad, resources hidden or known. Where you're starting matters, but forward is the direction that counts.

Get your journal, your most comfortable chair, maybe a favorite mug. Take a deep breath. Invite God to open your eyes, quiet your fears, and nudge you onward.

- Who are you - underneath the hats, tasks, or titles?
- What would it mean to thrive, not just survive, this season?
- How is God calling you toward greater joy, health, and service?

Let's move forward together. The world needs what only you can offer, and, my friend, the journey is far richer when it's shared.

You now understand the framework and the journey ahead. But understanding alone isn't transformation - it requires that crucial moment when you stop planning and start moving. Every great journey begins with a single step, and for many of us, that step has been waiting patiently for us to get "a round tuit."

Chapter 1: A Round Tuit

"The unexamined life is not worth living."
~Socrates, Apology (399 BC)

When I was growing up, I loved seeing my mom's sense of humor pop itself into a normal day. Being the fifth of six kids born to our family, I didn't get to see it enough. Life certainly can get busy and even difficult at times, especially when you have that many kids and a few of them have entered their teen years.

Mom was a deeply talented person. She had the most amazing touch when playing her prized Steinway parlor grand piano. She could be in the laundry room washing yet another load of laundry or perhaps reading the newspaper while sitting in her "Mrs." chair, as she called it, and without provocation, a song would come to her mind, causing her to go to her Steinway and fill our home with resounding melodies of her lifetime as she sang along.

A couple years ago, the church we had attended as a family for decades celebrated their 100th anniversary with a weekend of festivities, and while Mom loved seeing all the old pictures and historical newspaper clippings and essays that were displayed on the walls, and talking to friends she had known for most of her life, she could hardly wait to sneak back to visit her trusted best friend –

the piano she played nearly every church service for 45-plus years. She found her way to the piano bench and began to play. The effects of her 92 years of life seemed to wash away as she filled the room with beautiful renditions of hymns that, in that moment, brought together her faith in God, her passion for music, her life's vocational calling, and the perfect opportunity to reminisce of all the wonderful memories attached to that piano.

The room that had been empty other than the two of us quickly began to fill up with many people who were drawn in from all over the church because they recognized her unique style and were so excited to hear her play the way she had for so many years. "I *knew* that had to be Betty playing!" is what we heard over and over as people came in. Mom's playing had always brought people together in such a way that it was as though time stood still. She played song after song, request after request, and no one wanted to her stop. That is one of my favorite memories of her.

Mom left behind many artistic creations, including at least twenty watercolor paintings, some stained glass suncatchers that she had to learn how to solder to do, and even an entire children's Christmas cantata she wrote completely on her own! She came up with the plot, the music for a 10-piece orchestra and piano, and even the scripts for all the characters! Her creative ingenuity was demonstrated through several mediums and continues to inspire anyone who sees these treasures or hears about her decision to begin learning how to play the violin at 75 years of age.

As for her sense of humor, I remember her coming home one day from a women's meeting, excited to show me that she had gotten a memento to remember the speaker's topic. As she told me all about the troubles that procrastination can cause in a person's life, she opened her hand so I could see the round, plastic, quarter-sized, red pog that was stamped with "TUIT" on one side. She said, "Do you get it??" as she laughed and laughed. "I can't say anymore that I'll do something when I get a-round to-it!" That memory still makes me smile. Like most creative people, Mom occasionally struggled with completing tasks she started.

An unfinished, multicolored stained-glass box sits prominently in Mom's glass curio next to her Steinway in my living room so I can remember the charming complexities she possessed. You see, the lack of gumption to get a-round to-it did hamper her at times, but she did leave an enduring, lovely impression on this world by being the creative person she was made to be.

Betty would tell you, given the chance, that everyone needs someone to give them a round tuit, like the speaker gave her. Everyone has things in their life that inhibit (or even prohibit) the expression of their individual identity and completion of the very things they were built to do in this one life we get. *But,* let's not use Betty's story to give us a frightened urgency to get our acts together by tomorrow morning. She wouldn't like that. Instead, let's remember two things:

1. The key to success is consistent, minute progress

2. Perfection is the enemy of success.

Defining Success

Stop here for a moment and think of the person you believe best epitomizes success. Really. Stop and think. Considering the fact that everyone is unique in their personality, strengths, and desires, how would you define success? What about a person would make you see them as a picture of success? Maybe when I asked you to think of a person, perhaps you instead thought of someone who hasn't succeeded in anything, as far as you can tell. That's helpful, too. To find your own clear definition of success, play around with an idea for a while, thinking of those who you admire, those you don't, and what qualities provide the parameters of success.

Society's definition of success can overwhelm all of us through the innumerable images and messages each of us encounters daily, and they usually began as a marketing campaign for some shiny new product. We are influenced from birth through commercials, textbooks, social networks, celebrities, and even family and close friends. I remember vividly my one-year-old son saying some of his first words as we drove down the street, passing a familiar sign. He made the association and repeated what he had heard on tv recently: "Taco Bell dong!" I could hardly believe it. While that particular example doesn't necessarily state a definition of success, it certainly showcases the influence media has.

Allow me to share my definition of success, and you can decide how much we agree. A successful person has peace about who they are *and who they aren't*, has intentionally decided their life's goal according to their passions and calling, and has set their path toward it. Prioritized above those is the most important aspect of success: using whatever influence you have to inspire, empower, and uphold the people within reach. Let me explain by telling you a story.

John Maxwell is a world-renown author, speaker, and leadership expert, and his definition of a leader is anyone with influence. When I heard him say that on a stage just forty or fifty feet in front of me at a financial coaching conference, it gave me quite the pause. In a matter of minutes, my entire perspective on leadership shifted. You see, I had been atop my soapbox for all the years prior, pushing back against the cultural pressure for everyone to be all the desired things: extroverted, articulate, left-brained, rich, strong, attractive, and a leader. I would say, "Not everyone is built to be in front of people. Who would follow? The world would just be full of a bunch of people trying to boss each other around!"

But Dr. Maxwell was right. One day recently, I had the privilege of witnessing a beautiful moment. A six-year-old girl noticed an older woman walking with her hands full, including a plate of food. She quickly put her own plate down and hurried up to the older woman and said, "May I help you with that, ma'am? I know sometimes you're a little wobbly." Graciously, the woman smiled and allowed the little one to practice empathy in a practical way, giving her the power to change the entire atmosphere in the room simply through her unassuming actions and tiny little voice. Unknowingly, this little one encouraged others by filling everyone's hearts with memories of all the good in the world. From her, we learn the power of influence and how to use it for the betterment of the people around us.

You see, success should not mean being wealthy or working 24/7 or being the CEO of a large company, and it does not come from having an easy life or knowing the right people. A person's level of success in life is equated with how well they used their unique identity and purpose to find fulfillment and positively impact the world. This requires intentionality and consistent progress, resilience, and seeing everything in life through the filter of their end goal.

Some of the most notable heroes of modern history have overcome extreme difficulties, determined to make a positive impact no matter how much effort it took. Abraham Lincoln is such an example. He was born in poverty, mostly self-educated, and endured the deaths of his beloved mother, sister, and two of his four sons, and yet, he chose deliberate diligence and kept going. "I do the very best I know how – the very best I can; and I mean to keep doing so until the end." His legacy lives on as an admirable example of tenacious focus on the important things, despite over-whelming circumstances. I doubt anyone would see him as anything but a success.

Finding Inspiration in Others

Who inspires you? Mind you, this is not the same question I asked before about your example of a successful person. It's possible the same person answers both questions, but this is an equally important question to ponder separately. A person who inspires you isn't just an example of success that you could follow, but rather, something about them lights a spark inside you that compels you to act. That person somehow has expressed something that resonates deeply with something in your core being. Whatever inspiring thing they have done or said or stood for probably closely resembles a component of who you are built to be, what you are built to do, or the goals you wish to accomplish.

Recognizing those you consider successful and gathering stories of people who inspire you is like Betty's round tuit.

If you take some time to contemplate why you admire them, you will begin to find traction in your goal of self-discovery. My mother inspires me because I share her core principles that give purposeful meaning to my life. Our "whys" are the same, but Betty and I are very differently gifted. I am not meant to be a duplicate of her. Nor was she meant to be like me. Knowing *that* she inspires me and *how* she does gives me better understanding of myself in the ways that we are the same and the ways we are different. The people who inspire you guide you to a certain point, and from there, that inspiration should be the momentum to develop your unique personality and structure your life accordingly. Now let's take this yet another step further.

Defining Success for Your Life

Earlier we discussed a general definition of success and how society helps shape it. Add to it the things that make you feel successful, whether someone sees it or not. What brings you satisfaction or a sense of accomplishment? Be careful to not think about these things in comparison to other people, because doing so would require decisions about who is better or worse for each one. Not only is this a waste of time, it robs a person of their satisfaction or sense of accomplishment and lessens their value as a person and the offerings they bring to society.

All too many times I hear people say they aren't good enough or there are so many people better at "it" than they are, thinking this is reasonable support for not developing that particular skill any further. Falling as prey to the thought that either something isn't worth doing unless you are the best at it in the world or that whatever you would produce has already been made by someone else shuts down the creativity that is meant to be used.

Remember the second of the two rules a couple pages ago? *Perfection is the enemy of success.* If we keep looking outside ourselves for the value of who we are or what we can bring to the table, we can't help but develop a judgment system to determine the hierarchy of people and what they contribute to society. The result is self-promoting pride (and therefore rejection of other people) or low self-esteem (and therefore weakens oneself and society as a whole) and isolation (a dangerous combination).

Let's limit looking outside ourselves only to finding inspirational people that spark action in us, being careful to focus on the inspiration, but not focus so long on the person as to turn that inspiration into jealousy, competitiveness, or a yearning for perfection.

A sense of fulfillment is found by learning your unique identity and being the best at it you possibly can. Each person – distinctly designed in personality, skill strength, and passion – is a much-needed puzzle piece for society to operate well.

Let's "Begin Within" in the next chapter and define those things that make you distinctly you.

Over the following chapters, we will use assume a metaphor of a person walking on a path toward a horizon. We will look for ways to heal and strengthen the person, repair and straighten the path, and fully define the horizon, making sure the path he's on is headed toward the desired horizon, and set up systems to protect and ensure his successful journey.

The decision to act is crucial, but action without direction can waste precious energy and create unnecessary frustration. Before charging ahead with enthusiasm, wisdom requires that we first understand where we currently stand. Just as a skilled navigator must know their present location before plotting a course, your transformation journey begins with honestly assessing your current stage of development. Where exactly are you right now in your growth across The Six Dimensions of Health & Wellness?

Journal Prompts

- Think of a person you believe truly epitomizes success. Why did you choose them? What traits or choices made caused their success?
- Who inspires you? Why? Does this have any reflection on who you are built to be, what you are built to do, or goals you wish to accomplish?
- What is your general definition of success? How would you define success for your life? Has media's impact positively or negatively affected society's definition of success?

Chapter 1 Summary

Key Concepts:

- Moving from intention to implementation
- Excellence as faithful stewardship of God-given gifts

Action Items:

- Identify your personal "round tuit" areas of procrastination
- Write a commitment statement to yourself
- Schedule specific times for growth work
- Create environmental triggers for action

Main Takeaway: The gap between knowing what to do and actually doing it is bridged by intentional commitment and practical systems for follow-through.

Chapter 2: Stages of Growth - Knowing Where You Are

"Progress is impossible without change, and those who cannot change their minds cannot change anything." ~George Bernard Shaw

You know your desired destination - a life of integrated wellness, authentic purpose, and meaningful contribution. That's why you bought this book and are diligently working through its exercises. But the landscape between where you are now and your desired destination can seem overwhelming in the chaotic flow of life. So, let's take the first step toward tackling this portion of the journey. In this chapter, we will explore questions such as: Where exactly are you right now? What does the next stage of your journey look like? How do you know if you're making genuine progress or just spinning your wheels?

The work in this particular chapter is thicker than the others, and it is an important foundation for the work that follows. This is where understanding the stages of holistic development becomes not just helpful but essential. Research in developmental psychology reveals that growth across multiple dimensions doesn't happen randomly or all at once but follows predictable patterns that can guide your journey and help you navigate challenges with greater wisdom and patience. Understanding these stages provides both the perspective to appreciate how far you've already come and the roadmap to continue moving forward with intention and hope.

Just as a skilled gardener knows that different plants require different care at different seasons, understanding your current stage of development across The Six Dimensions of Health & Wellness enables you to apply the right strategies at the right time, preventing both discouragement from unrealistic expectations and stagnation from inadequate challenge.

The Science of Developmental Stages

The concept that human development occurs in predictable stages has deep roots in psychology, from Erik Erikson's psychosocial development theory to Abraham Maslow's hierarchy of needs. Modern academia has confirmed and refined these insights, revealing that growth across multiple dimensions of wellness follows identifiable patterns that can be measured, understood, and leveraged for more effective personal development.

Holistic Development Research: Optimal human development occurs when multiple dimensions (note: not *all*) are addressed simultaneously rather than in isolation. Dr. Bill Hettler and others have done work that supports the efforts to understand and actively work on multiple dimensions does indeed increase overall life satisfaction and more sustainable growth patterns than those who focus on single dimensions.

The Neuroscience of Staged Growth: Brain imaging reveals that different types of growth activate different neural networks and require different cognitive and emotional resources. This means that attempting to grow in *all areas simultaneously* at maximum intensity can actually slow progress by overwhelming our neurological capacity for change. Understanding developmental stages helps optimize our growth efforts by focusing energy where it will have the greatest impact at each phase.

The Four Primary Stages of Integrated Wellness

Based on decades of research in wellness psychology and validated through assessment tools used with thousands of individuals, we can identify four primary stages that characterize the journey toward integrated health and wellness. Understanding these stages helps you accurately assess where you are, celebrate appropriate progress, and focus your energy on the next logical steps.

As you read through these stages, remember this is a generalized, time-tested framework to use thoroughly but hold open-handedly. Much like Alcoholics Anonymous encourages their participants, let's remember to "take what you like and leave the rest." Humans rarely fit into a mold perfectly, and this framework is meant to provide lots of thought and fuel for your journey through chapter 11 and beyond.

Stage 1: Desert (Crisis and Awakening)

Characteristics: This stage is marked by significant neglect or crisis in one or more wellness dimensions, often accompanied by the recognition that current life patterns are unsustainable. People in the Desert stage frequently experience "rock bottom" moments that create both the pain necessary for change and the motivation to seek better approaches.

Common Indicators:

- Extreme neglect in critical areas (health crisis, relationship breakdown, spiritual emptiness, financial disaster)
- High stress levels with poor coping strategies
- Feelings of being overwhelmed, stuck, or hopeless
- Recognition that current life patterns aren't working
- Openness to significant change despite uncertainty about direction

Psychological Dynamics: The Desert stage often involves what psychologists call "cognitive dissonance" - the uncomfortable tension between current reality and desired outcomes. This tension, while painful, provides the motivational energy necessary for substantial change. Experiencing significant crisis often opens the door for greater capacity for transformation than attempting change from comfortable positions.

Integration Focus: The primary task at this stage is stabilization and safety. Attempting to grow in multiple dimensions simultaneously while in crisis typically leads to overwhelm and abandonment of growth efforts. Instead, individuals in the Desert stage benefit most from:

- **Immediate Crisis Management**: Addressing the most urgent threats to safety, health, or stability
- **Basic Need Fulfillment**: Ensuring adequate nutrition, sleep, shelter, and social support
- **Professional Support**: Often requiring counseling, medical attention, or financial guidance
- **Small, Manageable Steps**: Building momentum through achievable daily practices
- **Community Connection**: Finding others who provide encouragement and practical support

Spiritual Significance: From a Christian perspective, the Desert stage often represents what the biblical tradition calls "the valley of the shadow of death" - seasons where God's presence feels distant but where His faithfulness becomes most essential. Many significant biblical figures experienced desert seasons that prepared them for greater calling and service. The Desert stage, while difficult, can become the foundation for authentic spiritual depth and reliance on God's grace.

Practical Steps for Desert Stage:

- **Focus on one dimension at a time**, usually starting with physical or emotional stabilization
- Establish basic daily routines that support safety and wellbeing
- Seek professional help without shame or delay
- Connect with supportive community (church, support groups, trusted friends)
- Practice simple spiritual disciplines (prayer, journaling, Scripture reading, worship)

- Avoid major life decisions until stability is established

Stage 2: Overgrown/Malnourished/ Neglected (Awareness and Initial Change)

Characteristics: This stage involves growing awareness of the connections between different life dimensions and initial attempts at holistic improvement. However, progress is often inconsistent, with periods of growth followed by setbacks, and significant imbalances between different wellness dimensions.

Common Indicators:

- Some areas of life are developing while others remain neglected
- Increased self-awareness about problems and potential solutions
- Inconsistent motivation and follow-through on growth goals
- Tendency to focus intensively on one area while ignoring others
- Frequent "false starts" and abandoned improvement efforts
- Growing recognition that all areas of life are connected

Psychological Dynamics: This stage involves "differentiation" - the process of recognizing and developing distinct aspects of identity and capability. People in this stage often experience what appears to be contradictory growth, excelling in some areas while struggling in others. This is normal and necessary for eventual integration.

The Challenge of Partial Success: One of the most difficult aspects of Stage 2 is that partial success in some areas can create false confidence that leads to neglect of other important dimensions. For example, someone might achieve significant physical fitness while their relationships deteriorate or develop spiritual discipline while ignoring financial responsibility. Sustainable wellness requires eventual attention to all dimensions.

Integration Focus: The primary task at this stage is building awareness of connections between dimensions and developing sustainable practices across multiple areas:

- **Cross-Dimensional Awareness**: Learning to see how problems in one area affect others
- **Habit Formation**: Establishing small, consistent practices rather than dramatic overhauls
- **Patience with Process**: Accepting that growth takes time and involves setbacks
- **Holistic Assessment**: Regular evaluation of progress across all six dimensions
- **Balanced Attention**: Avoiding hyperfocus on single areas at the expense of others

Common Growth Areas: Stage 2 often focuses on initial progress in these patterns:

- Emotional awareness and basic emotional regulation skills
- Mental habits being formed in an environment redesigned for health across all dimensions
- Physical health improvements (exercise, nutrition, sleep)
- Spiritual exploration and establishment of basic practices

- Career or educational advancement
- Initial relationship improvements or new social connections
- Basic financial management and planning

Practical Steps for Stage 2:

- Use the Six Dimensions assessment tools regularly to maintain balanced perspective
- Start with small, daily practices rather than major lifestyle overhauls
- Create accountability systems for consistent progress
- Join groups or communities that support holistic growth
- Celebrate small wins while staying committed to long-term development
- Address obvious imbalances before they become crisis points

Stage 3: Surviving (Stability and Skill Building)

Characteristics: This stage represents solid functioning across most wellness dimensions with clear evidence of growth and stability. People in the Surviving stage have developed effective strategies for managing challenges and maintaining progress, though they may still lack the advanced skills and integrated approach characteristic of thriving.

Common Indicators:

- Basic needs are met across all six dimensions
- Consistent daily practices that support wellness

- Effective coping strategies for stress and setbacks
- Stable relationships and social support systems
- Clear sense of values and direction
- Growing confidence in ability to handle challenges
- Recognition of areas still needing growth but not feeling overwhelmed by them

Psychological Dynamics: Stage 3 involves what developmental psychologists call "consolidation" - the process of integrating and stabilizing gains made in previous stages. People in this stage often experience decreased emotional volatility and increased sense of personal efficacy compared to earlier stages.

The Platform Stage: Stage 3 functions as a platform for significant contribution to others. People who achieve basic stability across multiple life dimensions have increased capacity for service, leadership, and positive impact on their communities. This stage often marks the transition from primarily receiving support to providing support for others' growth.

Integration Focus: The primary task at this stage is skill building and preparation for expanded contribution:

- **Advanced Skill Development**: Moving beyond basic competence to expertise in key areas
- **Leadership Preparation**: Developing abilities to guide and support others
- **Vision Expansion**: Clarifying long-term goals and contribution aspirations
- **Resource Building**: Accumulating resources (financial, relational, knowledge) for future service
- **Mentoring Readiness**: Beginning to share wisdom and support others' growth

Common Growth Characteristics:

- **Emotional Maturity**: Advanced emotional intelligence and regulation skills; spiritual depth, mature faith practices, and growing wisdom
- **Mental Health & Habits:** Continuous learning and expertise development; structured life with margin built in
- **Physical Vitality**: Sustained energy and health that supports active lifestyle
- **Vocational Competence**: Career advancement and professional recognition; mentoring those younger in the field
- **Social Leadership**: Taking initiative in relationships and community involvement
- **Financial Wellness**: Wise use of resources, not used to salve maladapted dimensions

Practical Steps for Stage 3:

- Focus on developing advanced skills rather than just maintaining basic practices
- Begin mentoring or supporting others in their growth journeys
- Take on leadership roles in areas aligned with your values and calling
- Expand your vision for contribution beyond personal improvement
- Invest in building resources (education, relationships, finances) for future service
- Develop specialization in areas where your unique gifts can make significant impact

Stage 4: Thriving (Mastery and Contribution)

Characteristics: This stage represents integrated excellence across all wellness dimensions with primary focus on using personal development as a platform for significant contribution to others' growth and community flourishing. People in the Thriving stage demonstrate "generative leadership" - the ability to create conditions that support others' development and success.

Common Indicators:

- High functionality across all six wellness dimensions (Emotional, Mental, Physical, Vocational, Social, Financial)
- Sustainable practices that maintain growth without excessive effort
- Clear sense of life purpose and mission
- Significant positive impact on others' lives and community wellbeing
- Integration of personal growth with service to larger purposes
- Ability to navigate challenges without being derailed from core commitments
- Recognition as someone who helps others achieve their potential

Psychological Dynamics: Stage 4 involves what positive psychologists call "eudaimonic wellbeing" - happiness that comes from meaningful activity and contribution rather than just personal pleasure or achievement. In reaching this stage, individuals report higher life satisfaction, better physical health, and greater resilience than those focused primarily on personal advancement.

The Generative Focus: The defining characteristic of Stage 4 is what developmental psychologist Erik Erikson called "generativity" - concern for establishing and guiding the next generation and contributing to the greater good of society. This goes beyond mentoring individuals to creating systems, organizations, and cultures that support widespread human flourishing.

Integration Focus: The primary task at this stage is leveraging integrated personal development for maximum positive impact:

- **System Creation**: Building organizations, programs, or initiatives that multiply your impact
- **Culture Influence**: Shaping environments and communities to support holistic development
- **Legacy Building**: Creating lasting contributions that will continue beyond your lifetime
- **Advanced Mentoring**: Developing other leaders who can extend your influence
- **Wisdom Sharing**: Teaching and writing to spread insights and knowledge
- **Resource Stewardship**: Managing significant resources for kingdom purposes

Common Contribution Areas:

- **Organizational Leadership**: Leading businesses, nonprofits, or ministries with kingdom values
- **Educational Impact**: Teaching, training, or developing curricula that transform lives
- **Community Development**: Creating or improving communities that support human flourishing
- **Cultural Influence**: Affecting broader cultural conversations through media, politics, or advocacy

- **Economic Impact**: Using business or financial resources to create positive change
- **Spiritual Leadership**: Serving in roles that support others' spiritual growth and community health

Practical Steps for Stage 4:

- Regularly assess how your personal growth serves larger purposes
- Invest significant time and resources in developing other leaders
- Create systems and structures that multiply your positive impact
- Take calculated risks for causes larger than personal advancement
- Maintain personal growth practices while focusing primarily on contribution
- Build legacy projects that will continue beyond your direct involvement

Transitions Between Stages: Navigating Change with Grace

Transitions between stages are often more challenging than the stages themselves. Understanding the dynamics of stage transitions can help you navigate these periods with greater patience and effectiveness

The Transition Process: Stage transitions typically involve four phases:

- denial (resistance to acknowledging need for change),
- resistance (struggle with required adjustments),

- exploration (trying new approaches), and
- commitment (embracing new stage characteristics).

Each phase requires different strategies and support systems.

Regression and Cycling: Remember, stage progression is rarely linear. Don't give in to discouragement if you experience cycling between stages or experience temporary setbacks during stress, crisis, or major life changes. This is normal and doesn't represent failure but rather the natural process of growth and adaptation.

Adaptation Strategies: Successful stage transitions require specific adaptation strategies:

- **Cognitive Adaptation**: Developing new ways of thinking about challenges and opportunities
- **Behavioral Adaptation**: Learning new skills and practices appropriate to the next stage
- **Social Adaptation**: Building relationships and support systems that match your developmental needs
- **Spiritual Adaptation**: Deepening faith practices and theological understanding as you grow

Support Systems for Transitions: People who successfully navigate stage transitions have strong support systems that include mentors, peers, coaches, and cheerleaders who understand the developmental process. These relationships provide both emotional support during difficult transitions and practical guidance for new stage requirements. We will explore these relationship types in detail in chapter 10.

Practical Application: Assessing Your Current Stage

To effectively use this developmental framework, you need accurate assessment of your current stage across The Six Dimensions of Health & Wellness. Self-assessment combined with feedback from trusted others provides the most accurate picture of developmental status.

Self-Assessment Framework

Dimensional Evaluation: For each of The Six Dimensions, honestly assess your current functioning:

Emotional Wellness

How well do you understand, express, and manage your emotions? Are your emotions helping you navigate life, or do they often overwhelm or confuse you?

- **Desert:** Frequently feel numb, out of touch with emotions, or regularly overwhelmed by feelings you don't understand. Emotional outbursts or "shutdowns" are common.
- **Overgrown/Malnourished:** Sometimes aware of emotions but struggle to name them or respond constructively. Swing between periods of numbness and intensity.
- **Surviving:** Can identify emotions and manage most emotional ups and downs with basic skills or support but occasionally get stuck in certain moods or cycles.

- **Thriving:** Regularly use emotions as helpful data; practice healthy expression, self-compassion, and support others' emotional journeys.

Mental Health & Habits

Are your thoughts, attitudes, and daily routines supporting your growth? Do you have patterns that keep you moving forward, or do you find yourself stuck in negative cycles?

- **Desert:** Feel trapped by toxic thought patterns or paralyzed by worry, stress, or lack of motivation; daily routines barely exist or are chaotic.
- **Overgrown/Malnourished:** Occasionally commit to healthy habits or positive thinking, but consistency is lacking; experience cycles of progress and setback.
- **Surviving:** Mostly maintain supportive thought patterns and routines, though you sometimes struggle under pressure or during transitions.
- **Thriving:** Thought life is engaged, hopeful, and adaptive; healthy routines are automatic, with flexibility to adapt as life shifts.

Physical Health

How do your body, nutrition, and energy levels sustain your life? Is your body a partner in your growth, or a source of pain, neglect, or anxiety?

- **Desert:** Ignoring health needs, struggling with chronic exhaustion or symptoms, rarely engaging in movement or healthy eating.

- **Overgrown/Malnourished:** Inconsistent healthy choices; efforts at movement, nutrition, or sleep are sporadic or motivated mainly by guilt.
- **Surviving:** Reasonable energy and stamina more days than not; some positive health routines but may neglect specific needs or preventative care.
- **Thriving:** Invested in physical care as a form of stewardship and worship; energy, movement, sleep, and nutrition feel integrated into daily life.

Vocational Wellness

Does your work - whether paid, unpaid, or educational - feel meaningful and aligned with your gifts? Are you cultivating your passions, skills, and ultimate calling?

- **Desert:** Feel disengaged, bored, trapped, or in conflict with your role; work lacks meaning or drains your energy.
- **Overgrown/Malnourished:** Pursuing some skill-building or sense of purpose, but often at odds with daily responsibilities or uncertain about long-term direction.
- **Surviving:** Current work (job, volunteering, education) aligns reasonably well with your gifts and values; have some growth opportunities and feel mostly engaged.
- **Thriving:** Deep sense of calling informs daily choices; actively use your skills to serve others and invest in ongoing related learning.

Social Wellness

Are your relationships energizing and supportive, or do they repeatedly drain or isolate you? Do you have healthy boundaries and satisfying connections?

- **Desert:** Marked by isolation, loneliness, or frequent toxic/conflictual interactions; difficulty forming or maintaining trust.
- **Overgrown/Malnourished:** Some good connections, but many relationships are shallow, sporadic, or source of frequent frustration.
- **Surviving:** Several strong, reliable relationships; able to communicate needs and set basic boundaries, though some connections could be improved.
- **Thriving:** Connected in supportive, mutually uplifting community; actively nurture new and existing relationships, contributing to others' well-being as well.

Financial Wellness

Do your finances support your values and goals, or cause ongoing stress and conflict? Are you able to plan, save, and give with purpose?

- **Desert:** Avoid or fear money decisions; may be in crisis mode or feel "stuck" under burdensome debt or circumstances.
- **Overgrown/Malnourished:** Attempts at budgeting, saving, or planning, but struggle with consistency or emotional spending.

- **Surviving:** Can meet needs, plan ahead, and manage giving/saving; finances generally stable but future planning may need strengthening.
- **Thriving:** Feel confident and proactive in money management; have clear goals, healthy boundaries, and a sense of financial freedom that supports your calling and the ability to bless others.

Overall Stage Identification:
After reflecting on each dimension, identify your primary stage - most of your ratings will likely cluster in one category, but you may notice exceptions. Use this as a guide for setting focused goals for the next season, and to prioritize which areas need the most attention or support.

Journal prompts:

- Which dimension(s) feel strongest for you? Which are most "in the desert" right now?
- What small next step could you take this week to move one area forward?
- Who could offer support or accountability as you work on your next growth area?

Remember: The goal is not perfection, but progress. Regular honest assessment across The Six Dimensions helps you keep growing from stuck to unstoppable, one clear step at a time.

Integration Assessment

Overall Stage Identification: Look for patterns across dimensions:

- If most dimensions are in Desert stage, your overall development is likely Desert stage
- If you have a mix of stages with most in Overgrown/Malnourished, that's likely your primary stage
- If most dimensions are Surviving with some Thriving characteristics, you're likely in transition
- If most dimensions demonstrate Thriving characteristics, you've likely reached Stage 4
- If the dimensions don't easily indicate an overall stage, use the average of the stages (desert = 1, overgrown = 2, surviving = 3, thriving = 4; add then divide by 6).

Transition Indicators: Look for signs that you're moving between stages:

- Feeling restless or dissatisfied with current approaches
- Sensing that old strategies aren't working as well
- Increasing opportunities for greater responsibility or contribution
- Growing awareness of areas needing development
- Changes in relationships as you outgrow some connections and seek others

Adaptive Strategies for Each Stage

Different stages require different strategies for optimal growth and effective transitions. Understanding these stage-specific approaches can dramatically improve your growth effectiveness and reduce unnecessary struggle. Remember, these are reliable templates, but they do not need to be obeyed strictly. Read through them all and take the helpful information wherever it may have been listed.

Desert Stage Strategies

Focus on Stabilization:

- Address immediate safety and crisis issues first
- Establish basic daily routines that support physical and emotional stability
- Seek professional help without delay or shame
- Build or reconnect with supportive community
- Practice simple, consistent spiritual disciplines

Avoid These Common Mistakes:

- Trying to change everything at once
- Comparing yourself to people in later stages
- Isolating yourself from others during crisis
- Making major life decisions during acute crisis periods
- Ignoring professional help due to pride or fear

Overgrown/Malnourished Stage Strategies

Focus on Balance and Consistency:

- Use regular assessment tools to maintain awareness of all six dimensions
- Develop small, sustainable practices rather than dramatic lifestyle changes
- Address obvious imbalances before they become crisis points
- Build accountability systems for consistent growth
- Celebrate small wins while maintaining long-term perspective

Avoid These Common Mistakes:

- Hyper-focusing on one dimension while neglecting others
- Abandoning efforts after initial setbacks
- Trying to achieve perfection rather than progress
- Comparing your timeline to others' apparent success
- Giving up on areas that feel particularly challenging

Surviving Stage Strategies

Focus on Skill Development and Vision Expansion:

- Move beyond basic competence toward expertise in key areas
- Begin taking leadership roles in areas aligned with your values

- Develop mentoring relationships both as mentee and mentor
- Expand your vision for contribution beyond personal improvement
- Build resources (education, relationships, finances) for future service

Avoid These Common Mistakes:

- Becoming complacent with current level of functioning
- Failing to prepare for greater responsibilities and contributions
- Avoiding leadership opportunities due to false humility
- Maintaining exclusively receiving relationships without giving back
- Limiting vision to personal advancement rather than community contribution

Thriving Stage Strategies

Focus on Legacy and System Creation:

- Leverage personal development for maximum positive impact on others
- Create systems, organizations, or initiatives that multiply your influence
- Invest significant time and resources in developing other leaders
- Take calculated risks for causes larger than personal advancement
- Build legacy projects that will continue beyond your direct involvement

Avoid These Common Mistakes:

- Neglecting personal growth practices in favor of external contribution
- Trying to control outcomes rather than faithfully stewarding opportunities
- Becoming prideful about achievements rather than grateful for grace
- Burning out by taking on more responsibility than sustainable
- Failing to develop successors who can continue and expand your work

Moving Forward: Your Developmental Journey

Understanding stages of development isn't about putting yourself in a box or feeling limited by current circumstances. Instead, it's about gaining the perspective necessary to move forward with wisdom, patience, and appropriate expectations. People who understand these developmental processes make more strategic choices, experience less discouragement during difficult periods, and ultimately achieve greater life satisfaction and contribution.

Embracing Your Current Stage: Whatever stage you're currently in, remember that it serves important purposes in your overall development. Desert stages develop dependence on God and compassion for others in crisis. Overgrown/Malnourished stages develop self-awareness and resilience. Surviving stages develop competence and leadership capacity. Thriving stages develop wisdom and generative impact. Each stage has unique gifts and necessary lessons.

Preparing for What's Next: Use your understanding of developmental stages to prepare wisely for what's ahead. If you're in Desert stage, focus on stabilization while maintaining hope for greater contribution later. If you're in Overgrown/Malnourished stage, work on balance and consistency while developing vision for future service. If you're in Surviving stage, build skills and resources while expanding your capacity for contribution. If you're in Thriving stage, focus on legacy and system creation while maintaining the practices that got you there.

The Long View: Remember that this is a lifelong journey. Most people cycle through different stages multiple times as they face new challenges, opportunities, and life circumstances. The path ahead is both challenging and promising. But, trust the process, embrace your current reality, and step forward with confidence that your growth serves not just your own flourishing but the flourishing of everyone whose lives you touch. You are exactly where you need to be to take the next faithful step toward becoming all that God has created you to be.

Chapter 2 Summary

Key Concepts:

- Transitions between stages are often more challenging than the stages themselves
- Regression and cycling between stages are normal, not failure

Stage	Key Indicators	Core Strategy
Desert	Crisis, neglect, overwhelm	Stabilize, crisis management
Overgrown/Neglect	Inconsistency, focus on one area	Build awareness, small steps
Surviving	Stability, basic wellness, growing skills	Develop advanced skills, leadership, expansion
Thriving	Mastery, contribution, integrated wellness	Maximize impact, mentor others

Action Items:

- Assess your current stage across each of The Six Dimensions of Health & Wellness
- Identify stage-appropriate strategies for your current development
- Adjust expectations and goals to match your developmental reality
- Build support systems appropriate for your stage

🎯 **Main Takeaway:** Understanding your developmental stage provides perspective for strategic growth choices and patience during challenging transitions.

Step #1 Begin Within

Chapter 3: Begin Within - The Foundation of Self-Awareness

"Knowing yourself is the beginning of all wisdom."
~Aristotle, Metaphysics (350 BC)

Just as my dad, Doc Pratt, believed that good medicine required understanding the whole patient - not just symptoms but the person carrying them - genuine personal growth demands we start with a comprehensive, compassionate assessment of who we are. This isn't about harsh self-criticism or shallow self-improvement tricks. It's about the kind of deep, gracious self-knowledge that becomes the foundation for everything else.

The Science of Self-Awareness: Why This Matters

Social psychology has spent decades unraveling what happens when we turn our attention inward. The landmark research of Shelley Duval and Robert Wicklund in 1972 gave us objective self-awareness theory, which revealed something profound: when we focus attention on ourselves, we automatically begin comparing who we are with who we believe we should be. This isn't vanity or narcissism - it's one of the most fundamental processes that separates us from other species and allows us to grow, change, and become more than we currently are.

What's fascinating is that self-awareness can be triggered by surprisingly simple things. Mirrors, video cameras, hearing recordings of our own voices, or even just feeling like we stand out in a crowd can shift us into this reflective state. When this happens, something remarkable occurs: our behavior starts aligning more closely with our personal values and standards. We become more authentic versions of ourselves, not because we're trying harder, but because we're more conscious of the gap between our ideals and our actions.

This is why journaling works. Why honest conversations with trusted friends matter. Why quiet moments of reflection aren't luxury but necessity. Self-awareness isn't just feeling good about yourself - it's the cognitive and emotional foundation that makes lasting change possible.

Your Unique Fingerprint: Understanding Individual Differences

Here's what decades of research in personality psychology have confirmed: you are genuinely, scientifically, measurably unique. Your personality - the consistent patterns in how you think, feel, and behave - is like a fingerprint. No two people share the exact same combination of traits, strengths, preferences, and quirks that make up who you are.

This isn't pop psychology or feel-good platitudes. It's data. Individual differences in personality predict how we'll handle stress, what motivates us, how we communicate, what careers will energize rather than drain us, and even how we prefer to learn and grow. Understanding your unique psychological makeup isn't self-indulgence - it's strategy.

Consider how this plays out in real relationships. Studies reveal that personality traits like extroversion and agreeableness significantly predict how we use social media, how we form friendships, and even how we experience loneliness. Your degree of conscientiousness affects not just whether you'll stick to your goals, but how you'll approach the process of setting them in the first place. Your level of openness to experience influences whether you'll thrive on change and novelty or prefer stability and routine.

This research matters because it means there's no one-size-fits-all approach to personal growth. The strategies that work brilliantly for your best friend might leave you feeling frustrated and defeated - not because you're doing it wrong, but because you're wired differently. Understanding these differences is the key to finding approaches that work with your nature rather than against it.

The Power and Promise of Personality Assessment

You've probably taken a personality test at some point - maybe for work, maybe out of curiosity, maybe because someone forwarded you a link with "You HAVE to take this!" Subject lines multiply rapidly in our inboxes. But what exactly are these assessments measuring, and why do some feel remarkably insightful while others leave us scratching our heads?

The science behind personality assessment rests on a fundamental insight: if personality traits are real and measurable, then well-designed instruments should be able to detect and describe them reliably. Think of it like taking your temperature - a good thermometer will give you consistent, accurate readings that help you understand your physical state. Similarly, valid personality assessments provide consistent, meaningful information about your psychological tendencies.

But here's where it gets interesting: not all assessments are created equal. The most scientifically robust personality measures meet several rigorous criteria:

Reliability means the test gives consistent results. If you took it today and again in two weeks (assuming nothing major changed in your life), you'd get similar scores. This consistency is crucial because it suggests the test is measuring something stable about you, not just your mood on a particular day.

Validity is even more important - it means the test actually measures what it claims to measure. A valid measure of extroversion, for example, should correlate with real-world behaviors like seeking social situations, enjoying parties, and feeling energized around people.

Cross-validation ensures that the patterns found in one group of people hold true for others. This prevents us from building assessments that only work for college students or middle-aged professionals or any other narrow group.

The beauty of well-designed personality assessments lies not in putting you in a box, but in giving you a more nuanced vocabulary for understanding your inner world. They help you recognize patterns you might have sensed but never articulated. They validate experiences you thought were just quirks. They explain why certain situations energize you while others drain you, why you connect easily with some people but struggle with others.

Three Pillars of Self-Knowledge

As we dive deeper into self-awareness, I want to focus on three areas that research consistently shows matter most for personal growth and life satisfaction. Think of these as the three legs of a sturdy stool - all three need to be strong for the whole structure to support you.

1. Identity and Core Self-Concept

Your identity is your answer to the question "Who am I?" But it's more complex than you might think. Healthy identity formation involves integrating multiple dimensions of yourself into a coherent, stable sense of self.

This process typically intensifies during adolescence but continues throughout life as we encounter new roles, relationships, and experiences. Each major life transition - graduation, marriage, parenthood, career changes, loss - offers opportunities to refine and deepen our self-understanding.

What makes identity formation particularly interesting from a social psychology perspective is how much it happens in relationship with others. We don't develop our sense of self in isolation. We discover who we are through interactions with family, friends, mentors, and communities. We try on different roles and see how they fit. We get feedback - sometimes welcome, sometimes not - about how others experience us.

This is why the Christian understanding of identity as "beloved children of God" is so psychologically profound. It provides a secure foundation that isn't dependent on performance, appearance, or achievement. When our core identity is rooted in God's unchanging love, we're free to explore, experiment, and grow without the fear that mistakes will threaten our worth.

Journal Prompts for Identity Exploration:

- When you were a child, what did you dream of becoming? What drew you to those aspirations?
- What roles do you currently play in life (parent, employee, friend, etc.)? Which feel most natural and energizing?
- What values are non-negotiable for you - the principles you wouldn't compromise regardless of the situation?
- How would your closest friends describe your personality? What would they say are your most distinctive qualities?

2. Emotional Intelligence and Self-Regulation

Emotional intelligence - the ability to recognize, understand, and effectively manage emotions in yourself and others - has emerged as one of the most important predictors of life success. It may be even more important than traditional intelligence for workplace performance, relationship satisfaction, and overall well-being professional.

Daniel Goleman's influential model breaks emotional intelligence into five key components, but let's focus on the two that are most fundamental to self-awareness:

Emotional Self-Awareness involves recognizing your emotions as they arise and understanding how they affect your thoughts and behavior. This sounds simple, but many people struggle to accurately identify their emotional states. We might know we feel "bad" or "stressed" but lack the vocabulary to distinguish between frustration, disappointment, anxiety, and anger. Each of these emotions provides different information and calls for different responses.

Self-Regulation is the ability to manage your emotions rather than being hijacked by them. This doesn't mean suppressing feelings or pretending they don't exist. Instead, it means acknowledging emotions while choosing how to respond thoughtfully rather than reactively.

Here's where the social psychology research gets particularly helpful: higher skill in emotional regulation tends to bring stronger relationships, more career success, and better physical health. They're also more resilient in the face of setbacks and more effective at helping others through difficult times

The Christian tradition offers profound resources for emotional regulation through practices like prayer, meditation, confession, and community support. These aren't just spiritual disciplines - they're evidence-based strategies for developing emotional intelligence. When we regularly bring our inner life before God and trusted others, we develop the self-awareness and emotional vocabulary that are crucial for mental health and relational success.

Practical Exercises for Emotional Intelligence:

- Keep an emotion journal for one week. Several times each day, pause and ask: "What am I

feeling right now?" Try to use specific emotion words rather than generic terms like "good" or "bad."
- Practice the STOP technique when you notice strong emotions: Stop what you're doing, Take a breath, Observe what you're feeling and thinking, Proceed with intention rather than reaction.
- Ask trusted friends for feedback about your emotional patterns. What do they notice about your typical responses to stress, conflict, or change?

3. Strengths, Talents, and Calling

One of the most significant shifts in psychology over the past few decades has been toward strengths-based approaches to human development. Rather than focusing primarily on fixing weaknesses, people flourish when they identify and develop their natural talents and abilities.

This aligns beautifully with a biblical understanding of gifts and calling. Scripture teaches that God has uniquely equipped each person with specific abilities meant to serve others and build up the community. From a psychological perspective, we can observe that people experience greater engagement, satisfaction, and effectiveness when their daily activities align with their natural strengths.

But here's what makes this particularly relevant for personal growth: your strengths aren't just what you're good at - they're activities that energize rather than drain you. You might be competent at many things, but your true strengths are the abilities that feel natural, that you can develop without enormous effort, and that leave you feeling alive rather than depleted.

Research on vocational psychology reveals that people who understand their strengths and find ways to use them regularly - whether in paid work, volunteer roles, or personal relationships - report higher levels of life satisfaction and lower levels of burnout and depression.

Questions for Strengths Discovery:

- What activities make you lose track of time because you're so absorbed in them?
- What compliments do you receive repeatedly? What do people regularly ask for your help with?
- Think of your most satisfying accomplishments. What strengths did you use to achieve them?
- What problems do you naturally notice and feel compelled to solve?
- What aspects of your current work or responsibilities energize you? What aspects drain you?

The Integration Challenge: Becoming Whole

Self-awareness isn't about collecting personality test results like trophies or becoming obsessed with self-analysis. The goal is integration - developing a coherent, compassionate understanding of yourself that enables authentic living and meaningful growth.

This integration happens best in community. While self-reflection is important, we also need the mirrors that healthy relationships provide. We need people who know us well enough to lovingly challenge our blind spots and affirm our growth. We need mentors who can help us see potential we might miss and peers who can share the journey of discovery.

Our self-concept is partly formed through reflected appraisals - how we think others see us. This means that surrounding ourselves with people who see us accurately and celebrate our authentic selves becomes crucial for healthy self-awareness.

From a Christian perspective, this community aspect of self-discovery reflects our fundamental design for relationship. We weren't meant to figure out life alone. The body of Christ functions precisely because different members bring different gifts, perspectives, and strengths. Your self-awareness contributes not just to your own flourishing but to the health of the whole community.

Moving Forward with Self-Compassion

As you begin this journey of deeper self-awareness, I want to offer you the same grace I hope you'll extend to yourself: you are a work in progress, beloved of God, with immense potential for growth and service. The goal isn't perfection but increasing authenticity and alignment between who you are and how you live.

Research on self-compassion - treating yourself with the same kindness you'd offer a good friend - shows that people who approach self-discovery with gentleness rather than harsh judgment are actually more likely to make positive changes and sustain them over time. When we're not afraid of what we might discover about ourselves, we're free to be honest about both our strengths and our areas for growth.

Remember that self-awareness is not a destination but an ongoing practice. As you change and grow, as your circumstances shift, as you encounter new challenges and opportunities, your understanding of yourself will deepen and evolve. The personality traits measured by assessments tend to remain relatively stable over time, but your capacity to understand, appreciate, and effectively use your unique design can continue growing throughout your life.

Your Next Steps in Self-Discovery

As we conclude this foundational chapter on beginning within, let me suggest some concrete steps you can take to deepen your self-awareness:

1. **Choose one personality assessment to complete thoughtfully.** Look for measures that have solid research support and take time to reflect on your results rather than just glancing at them.
2. **Begin a regular practice of self-reflection.** This might be daily journaling, weekly walks for contemplation, or monthly conversations with a trusted friend or mentor about your growth and insights.
3. **Ask for feedback from people who know you well.** Choose individuals who care about your growth and can offer both affirmation and gentle challenge.
4. **Pay attention to your energy patterns.** Notice what activities, relationships, and environments energize you versus drain you. These patterns offer important clues about your authentic self.
5. **Practice emotional vocabulary building.** Try to name your emotions specifically rather than using

general terms. The more precise your emotional awareness, the better equipped you'll be to respond rather than react.

The ancient Greek maxim "know thyself" remains as relevant today as it was thousands of years ago. But now we know from psychological research exactly why self-knowledge matters so much: it's the foundation for emotional regulation, authentic relationships, meaningful work, and sustained personal growth. It's the starting point for becoming who God created you to be.

As we prepare to move forward to building solid footing for your journey, take a moment to appreciate the courage it requires to look honestly at yourself. This kind of self-examination isn't always comfortable, but it's always worthwhile. You are fearfully and wonderfully made, with a unique combination of traits, gifts, and experiences that the world needs. The better you understand this unique design, the more effectively you can offer your authentic self in service to others and glory to God.

In the next chapter, we'll explore how to take this foundational self-knowledge and use it to establish the solid footing you'll need for lasting change. But for now, rest in the assurance that the journey of self-discovery is itself a sacred act - a way of honoring the God who created you with such intentionality and care.

Journal Prompts:

- How has your understanding of yourself changed over the past year?
- What aspect of your personality do you most appreciate? What aspect challenges you the most?
- In what ways do you see God's design and purpose reflected in your unique traits and abilities?
- What would it look like for you to live more authentically in your current circumstances?
- How might deeper self-awareness enable you to serve others more effectively?

Take your time with these questions. Let them simmer. Share them with trusted friends. Most importantly, approach them with the same grace and curiosity you'd bring to getting to know any beloved person. Because that's exactly what you're doing - getting to know the beloved person God created you to be.

Chapter Three Summary

📋 Key Concepts:

- Objective self-awareness theory and its psychological benefits
- Three pillars: Identity/self-concept, emotional intelligence, and strengths/calling
- Personality assessment science and validity factors
- Self-awareness as ongoing practice, not one-time achievement

⚡ Action Items:

- Complete a research-validated personality assessment
- Begin daily emotion journaling with specific emotion words
- Conduct values clarification exercise
- Ask trusted friends for feedback on your strengths and blind spots

🎯 **Main Takeaway:** Self-awareness is the foundation for all authentic growth - knowing who God created you to be enables you to become more fully that person.

Step #2
Solid
Footing

Chapter 4: Solid Footing - One Step at a Time

"Success is the sum of small efforts repeated day in and day out." ~Robert Collier

Now that you've begun the essential work of self-discovery, we need to channel that deepening self-awareness into something concrete and actionable. Think of it this way: knowing yourself is like having a detailed map of your unique terrain - your personality, strengths, values, and calling. But a map alone doesn't get you anywhere. You need to decide where you're going and plot a course that honors both your authentic design and your desired destination.

This is where many well-intentioned personal growth journeys stall. We attend workshops, read books, take assessments, and gain wonderful insights about ourselves, but then struggle to translate those revelations into lasting change. The gap between self-knowledge and sustained transformation is bridged by what we'll explore in this chapter: building the solid footing of values-based decision making, meaningful goal setting, and the psychological foundations that support long-term commitment.

The Foundation of Values-Based Living

Here's what decades of psychological research have confirmed about values: they are among the most powerful predictors of human behavior, more influential than personality traits, circumstances, or even immediate emotions. Your core values - those principles you hold most dear - act like an internal compass, guiding decisions even when the path ahead is unclear or difficult.

But here's where it gets interesting from a social psychology perspective. Brain imaging technology reveals that when people make decisions aligned with their core values, specific neural regions associated with reward processing become more active. In other words, living according to your values doesn't just feel right morally or spiritually - it literally activates the brain's reward circuits, creating a neurobiological foundation for sustained motivation and well-being.

This is profound because it means that values-based decision making isn't just about being "good" or principled. It's about creating a life structure that works with, rather than against, how your brain is designed to experience satisfaction and meaning. When your daily choices consistently align with your deepest convictions, you're not just following rules - you're activating the very neural pathways that support long-term happiness and resilience.

Consider how this plays out practically. Research on value-based decision-making shows that people who regularly consult their core values when facing choices report higher life satisfaction, less decision fatigue, and greater confidence in their choices, even when those choices involve short-term sacrifice. They also demonstrate more consistent behavior over time, because their decisions arise from stable internal principles rather than shifting external circumstances or momentary impulses.

Understanding the Science of Goal Setting

If values provide your compass, goals become your roadmap. But not all goal setting is created equal, and this is where psychological research offers crucial insights that can save you years of frustration and false starts.

Edwin Locke and Gary Latham established what's now called Goal Setting Theory, which reveals four key mechanisms that explain why specific types of goals dramatically improve performance. When goals are properly structured, they direct attention toward relevant activities, increase effort, enhance persistence, and promote the development of effective strategies. These aren't just feel-good concepts - they're measurable psychological processes that can be leveraged for transformation.

But here's where recent research has added important nuance: the effectiveness of specific goal-setting approaches depends significantly on what you're trying to accomplish and where you are in the learning process. For novel or complex tasks, overly specific goals can actually hinder performance by constraining exploration and learning. However, for familiar tasks or areas where you're building on existing skills, specific goals consistently outperform vague intentions.

This is particularly relevant for personal growth because transformation typically involves both elements: learning new ways of thinking and behaving (where flexibility may be beneficial) and consistently applying familiar principles (where specificity drives results).

The most robust support exists for what's commonly known as SMART goals - Specific, Measurable, Achievable, Relevant, and Time-bound. While this framework has limitations, particularly in healthcare and complex personal development contexts, it provides a useful starting structure that can be adapted based on your specific growth areas.

The Psychology of Effective Goal Setting:

Direction and Focus: Well-constructed goals act like a spotlight, directing your attention toward activities that move you forward and away from distractions that don't serve your growth. This isn't just about willpower - it's about leveraging your brain's natural tendency to focus on what you've explicitly identified as important.

Effort Amplification: Challenging (but achievable) goals lead to higher levels of effort than easy or vague goals. When you set a goal that requires genuine stretching, your brain automatically allocates more cognitive and emotional resources toward achieving it.

Persistence Through Difficulty: Perhaps most importantly, clear goals extend the time you're willing to invest in pursuit of an outcome. When obstacles arise - and they always do - people with well-defined goals demonstrate greater resilience and staying power.

Strategic Thinking: The process of setting meaningful goals naturally promotes strategic thinking. Instead of hoping change will happen, you begin developing specific approaches, identifying potential barriers, and creating contingency plans.

The Power of Intrinsic Motivation

This brings us to one of the most important distinctions in motivational psychology: the difference between intrinsic and extrinsic motivation. Self-Determination Theory, developed by Edward Deci and Richard Ryan, reveals that people are most engaged, persistent, and satisfied when their goals serve three fundamental psychological needs: autonomy (feeling in control of your choices), competence (experiencing mastery and effectiveness), and relatedness (connecting meaningfully with others).

Goals that emerge from these intrinsic motivations - personal growth, meaningful relationships, contributing to something larger than yourself - tend to be more sustainable than goals driven primarily by external rewards like money, status, or approval. This isn't to say external motivations are unimportant, but when intrinsic and extrinsic motivations align, people experience greater satisfaction and are more likely to persist through challenges.

From a Christian perspective, this psychological truth beautifully supports what Scripture teaches about calling and purpose. When our goals are rooted in love for God and service to others - intrinsic motivations at their highest level - we tap into sources of energy and persistence that external rewards alone cannot provide. The joy found in living according to God's design for us isn't just spiritual truth; it's also psychological reality.

Practical Application: When setting goals for your growth journey, ask yourself not just "What do I want to achieve?" but "Why does this matter to me personally?" and "How will accomplishing this enable me to serve others more effectively?" Goals that answer these deeper questions of purpose tend to be more motivating and sustainable over time.

Building Commitment: The Psychology of Follow-Through

Knowing what you want to accomplish is only the beginning. The psychological literature on commitment reveals why some people consistently follow through on their intentions while others struggle with the "intention-action gap".

Commitment, from a psychological perspective, involves both dedication (emotional attachment and personal investment) and constraint (factors that make abandoning a goal costly or difficult). The most successful long-term changers cultivate both dimensions, creating both internal motivation and external structures that support persistence.

The Role of Identity in Commitment: Our deepest commitments are those that align with our sense of identity. When achieving a goal becomes part of how you see yourself - "I am someone who keeps their word," "I am someone who cares for their health," "I am someone who serves others" - following through becomes not just something you do but something that expresses who you are.

This is why the self-awareness work from our previous chapter is so crucial. The better you understand your authentic identity, the easier it becomes to set goals that feel genuinely connected to who you are rather than who you think you should be.

Environmental Design for Success: Commitment research also emphasizes the importance of environmental factors. People who successfully maintain long-term changes typically create external structures - accountability partners, scheduled check-ins, visible reminders, modified environments - that make persistence easier and abandonment more difficult.

This isn't about lacking willpower; it's about working intelligently with human psychology. Your brain is constantly scanning for cues about what matters most, and a well-designed environment sends consistent signals that support rather than undermine your commitments.

Grit, Growth Mindset, and the Long View: The Doc Pratt Principle

Two concepts from positive psychology deserve special attention as we build solid footing for lasting change: grit and growth mindset.

Grit: Passion and Perseverance for Long-Term Goals

Angela Duckworth's work on grit - defined as passion and perseverance in pursuit of long-term goals - has revealed that this quality is often a better predictor of success than talent, intelligence, or favorable circumstances. Grit involves two key components: maintaining effort despite failures and obstacles, and maintaining interest despite boredom, distractions, or lack of progress.

What makes grit particularly relevant for personal transformation is that it can be developed. Grittier individuals aren't necessarily born with more persistence - they cultivate specific habits and mindsets that support long-term pursuit of meaningful goals.

The Christian concept of perseverance aligns beautifully with grit research. Scripture repeatedly emphasizes the importance of persistence in the face of difficulty, not as grinding determination but as faithful endurance rooted in hope and purpose. When our long-term goals serve God's kingdom and our authentic calling, we tap into sources of grit that extend far beyond personal willpower.

Growth Mindset: The Belief in Development

Carol Dweck's findings on mindset reveals that people who believe abilities can be developed through effort and learning (growth mindset) tend to embrace challenges, persist through setbacks, and ultimately achieve higher levels of performance than those who believe abilities are fixed traits (fixed mindset).

Recent studies have added important nuance to mindset theory. Simply adopting a growth mindset isn't magic - the effects depend heavily on context, the specific domain, and how mindset interventions are implemented. However, when properly understood and applied, growth mindset can significantly enhance learning, resilience, and long-term development.

For personal transformation, growth mindset is crucial because change inherently involves learning new ways of thinking and behaving. When you approach your growth journey with confidence that you can develop new capacities - rather than believing you're limited by current abilities - you're more likely to persist through the inevitable frustrations that come with learning.

Integration Point: The research on grit and growth mindset converges on a powerful truth: lasting change requires both believing in your capacity to grow and committing to sustained effort over time. Neither belief nor effort alone is sufficient, but together they create a foundation for transformation that can weather the storms of difficulty and discouragement.

Faith-Informed Goal Setting: Where Psychology Meets Spiritual Formation

As we integrate psychological insights with Christian living, it's important to recognize that goal setting isn't just about personal achievement - it's about stewardship. The parable of the talents teaches that we're accountable for developing and using what God has entrusted to us. From this perspective, setting meaningful goals becomes an act of faithful stewardship rather than self-centered ambition.

Praying Through Your Goals: Before we get to practical exercises, consider how prayer can inform your goal-setting process. Bringing your aspirations before God isn't just about asking for blessing on your plans - it's about aligning your desires with His purposes and seeking wisdom about how to steward your life well.

Community Discernment: Biblical wisdom also emphasizes the importance of community in discerning direction. Proverbs reminds us that plans succeed through many advisers. As you set goals for your growth, involve trusted Christian friends, mentors, or spiritual directors who can offer perspective, encouragement, and accountability.

Practical Framework: Building Your Solid Footing

Now let's translate these research insights into concrete steps for establishing solid footing in your transformation journey.

Step 1: Clarify Your Core Values

Values Assessment Exercise: Find this assessment in Appendix A. Follow the instructions there and return here.

What themes emerge about what matters most deeply to you? Consider both your natural inclinations and your spiritual convictions. What principles would you want to guide your decisions even if no one was watching?

The most influential values are those that integrate both personal authenticity and transcendent purpose. In Christian terms, these are values that honor both how God made you uniquely and how He calls you to serve others.

Values Integration: Once you've identified your core values, the next step is integration - consistently using these values to guide decisions both large and small. Start with lower-stakes choices and build the habit of values-based decision making before applying it to major life decisions.

Step 2: Set Learning-Oriented Goals

Based on the latest academic observations on goal effectiveness, consider setting both specific performance goals (for areas where you're building on existing skills) and learning goals (for areas where you're developing new capacities).

Performance Goals: "I will spend 30 minutes in prayer and Scripture reading each morning before checking email." (Specific, measurable, building on existing spiritual practices)

Learning Goals: "I will explore what it means to practice hospitality in my current life circumstances." (Open-ended, focusing on discovery rather than specific metrics)

Growth-Oriented Framing: Frame your goals in terms of development rather than fixed outcomes. Instead of "I will be more patient," try "I will develop greater capacity for patience through daily practice of [specific strategies]."

Step 3: Design Supporting Environments

Environmental Audit: Look at your physical and social environments. What cues currently support or undermine the changes you want to make? How can you modify your surroundings to make good choices easier and poor choices more difficult?

Accountability Structures: Sharing goals with supportive others within the social group makes achieving them much more likely. Who in your life could serve as encouragers and accountability partners for your growth goals?

Rhythm and Routine: Design regular rhythms that support your growth goals. The power isn't in perfection but in consistency. Small, regular actions aligned with your values create momentum over time.

Step 4: Cultivate Intrinsic Motivation

Connection to Purpose: Regularly remind yourself why your goals matter. How do they serve your calling? How do they enable you to love God and neighbor more fully? Connecting actions to deeper purposes maintains motivation longer.

Celebrate Process, Not Just Outcomes: Growth mindset research suggests celebrating effort, learning, and progress rather than just final achievements. This keeps motivation alive during the long middle of pursuing meaningful goals.

Step 5: Plan for Obstacles

Implementation Intentions: Create "if-then" plans for when potential obstacles are significantly more likely to persist as difficulties arise. "If I feel discouraged about my progress, then I will review my list of reasons why this goal matters and call my accountability partner."

Grit Development: Identify what gives you energy for long-term pursuit. What reminders, practices, or relationships help you maintain perspective when progress feels slow? Build these grit-supporting elements into your regular routines.

The Integration Challenge: From Knowledge to Living

As we conclude this chapter on building solid footing, remember that the goal isn't perfection in goal setting but rather developing the capacity to consistently align your actions with your values and calling. Transformation happens through sustained effort directed toward meaningful ends, not through dramatic one-time changes or perfect planning.

The solid footing we're building isn't meant to be rigid but rather stable enough to support growth while flexible enough to adapt as you learn and develop. Like a well-rooted tree that can bend without breaking in strong winds, the foundation we're establishing should provide both stability and resilience.

Your values serve as roots - drawing nourishment from your deepest convictions and God's purposes for your life. Your goals serve as branches - reaching toward specific areas of growth and service. Both are necessary for a healthy, flourishing life that can weather seasons of difficulty and bear fruit that serves others.

Moving Forward: From Solid Footing to Clear Obstacles

In our next chapter, we'll examine the hindrances - those often-unconscious forces that can derail even the most well-intentioned growth efforts. But for now, take time to establish the solid footing that will support you through the challenges ahead.

Journal Prompts:

- What core values emerged from your self-awareness work? How do these align with your understanding of how God has designed and called you?
- What's one area where you sense God calling you to growth? How might you frame this as both a specific goal and a learning journey?
- What environmental changes could you make to better support the person you're becoming?
- Who in your life could serve as encouragers and accountability partners for your growth goals?
- What obstacles do you anticipate in pursuing your goals? How might you prepare for these challenges in advance?
- How can you regularly remind yourself of the deeper purposes that motivate your growth goals?

The foundation you're building now - rooted in self-awareness, guided by values, directed by meaningful goals, and supported by commitment - will serve you well in the journey ahead. Change is never easy, but with solid footing established, you're equipped not just to survive the challenges of transformation but to thrive through them.

As you continue forward, remember that this isn't ultimately about self-improvement but about becoming more fully the person God created you to be, equipped and empowered to serve His kingdom and love others well. That's a foundation that can support any dream and weather any storm.

Chapter 4 Summary

Key Concepts:

- Values-based decision making activates brain reward circuits
- SMART goals vs. learning goals for different situations
- Self-determination theory: autonomy, competence, relatedness
- Grit and growth mindset as learnable skills

Action Items:

- Create your core values statement
- Set both performance and learning goals
- Design environmental supports for your goals
- Develop "if-then" implementation intentions for obstacles

Main Takeaway: Sustainable change comes from aligning actions with authentic values through well-designed goals supported by environmental changes and community accountability.

Step #3 Hindrances

Chapter 5: Hindrances - Invisible Forces That Shape Us

"Until you make the unconscious conscious, it will direct your life, and you will call it fate."
~Carl Jung

There's a story that's been passed down through generations, though its exact origins remain unclear. A young woman, newly married, was preparing her first holiday roast for her husband's family. As she began her preparations, she carefully cut about two inches off each end of the roast before placing it in the pan. Her husband, watching curiously, asked, "Honey, why did you cut the ends off the roast?"

"Well," she replied, "that's how my mother always did it. It must be the secret to making it taste better."

Intrigued, the husband called his mother-in-law. "Mom, can you tell us why you always cut the ends off the roast before cooking it?"

The mother paused, then laughed. "Oh, that! I only did that because my roasting pan was too small for the whole roast. I had to cut it to make it fit."

This simple story illustrates one of the most profound challenges we face in personal transformation: the invisible forces that shape our decisions, beliefs, and behaviors without our conscious awareness. These hindrances don't announce themselves with fanfare or warning labels. Instead, they operate in the shadows of our psyche, quietly directing our choices and limiting our potential while we remain blissfully unaware of their influence.

Social psychology has spent decades studying these unconscious forces, revealing how powerfully they shape human behavior. What we're discovering is both humbling and hopeful: humbling because it reveals how much of our decision-making happens below the level of conscious awareness, and hopeful because once we understand these patterns, we can begin to choose more intentionally which influences to embrace and which to challenge.

The Science of Unconscious Influence

Cognitive psychology has revealed that the human brain processes approximately 11 million bits of information per second, yet we can only consciously attend to about 40 bits at any given moment. This means that 99.99% of the information influencing our thoughts and behaviors operates below the threshold of conscious awareness. Our brains have sophisticated systems for making rapid decisions based on patterns, assumptions, and shortcuts - what psychologists call heuristics - that help us navigate the world efficiently but don't always serve us well.

These unconscious processes aren't inherently problematic. They allow us to function in a complex world without being overwhelmed by every stimulus and decision. The challenge arises when these automatic patterns become rigid, outdated, or misaligned with our conscious values and goals. What served as protective or adaptive responses in one context may become limiting beliefs in another.

Daniel Kahneman's groundbreaking research on "System 1" and "System 2" thinking helps us understand this dynamic. System 1 operates automatically and quickly, with little conscious effort, drawing on stored patterns and past experiences to make instant judgments. System 2 involves more deliberate, logical, and effortful mental activity. While System 1 is incredibly efficient, it's also susceptible to biases and can perpetuate patterns that no longer serve us.

From a Christian perspective, this psychological truth aligns with Scripture's recognition that we don't always understand our own hearts or motivations. Jeremiah 17:9 reminds us that "the heart is deceitful above all things and beyond cure. Who can understand it?" This isn't condemnation but rather acknowledgment of our need for divine insight and community wisdom to see ourselves clearly and make choices aligned with God's purposes rather than merely our unconscious patterns.

Generational Transmission: The Long Echo of the Past

One of the most powerful sources of unconscious influence comes through generational transmission - the ways that beliefs, behaviors, and even trauma pass from one generation to the next, often without explicit teaching or awareness.

The field of epigenetics has revealed that *traumatic experiences can actually alter gene expression in ways that affect not just the trauma survivor but their children and grandchildren.* Studies of Holocaust survivors and their descendants, for example, have found specific epigenetic markers related to stress response that persist across generations, even in family members who never experienced the original trauma directly.

But generational transmission isn't limited to trauma. Patterns of thinking, relating, and problem-solving are also passed down through families and communities through both explicit teaching and implicit modeling. Children learn not just what parents say but how parents handle stress, navigate relationships, make decisions, and understand themselves in the world.

The Roast Story Revisited: The young woman in our opening story wasn't just following a cooking technique - she was unconsciously perpetuating a problem-solving approach passed down through her family. Without questioning or examining the underlying reasons, she accepted that "this is how we do things" as sufficient justification for her behavior.

Consider how this plays out in more consequential areas of life:

- **Relationship patterns**: If you grew up in a household where conflict was avoided at all costs, you might find yourself automatically withdrawing from healthy confrontation in your marriage, even when direct communication would serve the relationship better.
- **Money beliefs**: Family messages about money - whether spoken or unspoken - often shape financial decisions decades later. "We can't afford that," "Money doesn't grow on trees," or "Rich

people are greedy" can become unconscious filters that limit financial growth and stewardship.
- **Career expectations**: Generational beliefs about work, education, and success can either launch or limit professional development. "People like us don't do that kind of work" or "Don't get too big for your britches" can become internal barriers to pursuing calling and gifting.
- **Spiritual practices**: Even our approaches to faith can be unconsciously inherited. We may practice Christianity the way we learned it without ever examining whether our inherited patterns align with Scripture or serve our spiritual growth.

Breaking Generational Patterns: The goal isn't to reject everything from previous generations - much of what we inherit is valuable and worth preserving. Rather, it's about making conscious choices about which patterns to continue and which to modify or release. This requires "mentalization" - the ability to understand behavior in terms of underlying mental states and motivations.

Cultural Conditioning: The Invisible Water We Swim In

Just as fish are unaware of the water they swim in, we're often unconscious of the cultural forces that shape our worldview, decision-making processes, and definitions of success, morality, and meaning.

The way people from different societies approach decision-making, relationships, and personal growth can be profoundly different. What feels "natural" or "right" to us is often the result of cultural conditioning rather than universal truth. Understanding these influences isn't about rejecting our cultural heritage but rather about making more intentional choices about which cultural values to embrace and which to challenge.

Individualism vs. Collectivism: Western cultures tend to emphasize individual achievement, personal responsibility, and self-reliance, while many other cultures prioritize community harmony, collective decision-making, and interdependence. Neither approach is inherently superior, but unconscious adherence to either extreme can create problems. *Excessive individualism can lead to isolation and burnout, while excessive collectivism can suppress authentic identity and calling.*

Time Orientation: Some cultures are highly future-oriented, emphasizing planning, goal-setting, and delayed gratification, while others are more present-oriented, valuing spontaneity, flexibility, and immediate relationships. Again, both orientations have strengths and limitations. The key is conscious awareness of your cultural conditioning and intentional choice about when each approach serves you well.

Success Definitions: Cultural messages about what constitutes a successful life profoundly influence our goals and life choices. In some contexts, success is measured primarily by financial achievement and individual accomplishment. In others, it's defined by community contribution, family harmony, or spiritual development. Christian culture adds another layer, sometimes emphasizing service and sacrifice while de-emphasizing material prosperity or personal fulfillment.

Decision-Making Styles: Significant differences in how decision-making is approached can be found between cultures. Some cultures value quick decisiveness, viewing indecision as weakness. Others emphasize thorough deliberation and consensus-building, viewing rushed decisions as reckless. Some cultures encourage challenging authority and questioning assumptions, while others prioritize respect for hierarchy and tradition.

The Integration Challenge: For Christians living in multicultural contexts, the challenge becomes even more complex. We must navigate the values of our ethnic or national culture, the subculture of our Christian community, and the broader secular culture, all while seeking to align our lives with biblical principles. This requires ongoing discernment about which cultural influences support spiritual growth and which create barriers to following Christ authentically.

Self-Limiting Beliefs: The Stories We Tell Ourselves

Perhaps the most personal category of unconscious hindrances involves the self-limiting beliefs we've developed about our own abilities, worth, and potential. These internal narratives often operate as self-fulfilling prophecies, shaping our behavior in ways that confirm the very limitations we believe about ourselves.

The Neuroscience of Belief Formation: Self-limiting beliefs literally rewire our brains through a process called neuroplasticity. When we repeatedly think thoughts like "I'm not good at public speaking" or "I'll never be financially secure," we strengthen the neural pathways associated with those beliefs, making them feel increasingly true and automatic. These beliefs then filter our perceptions, causing us to notice evidence that confirms them while overlooking contradictory information.

Common Sources of Self-Limiting Beliefs:

Childhood Experiences: Early messages from parents, teachers, siblings, and peers can become internalized truths that persist into adulthood. A teacher's offhand comment about math ability, a parent's frustrated exclamation during a stressful moment, or classmates' teasing can plant seeds that grow into limiting beliefs decades later.

Past Failures or Traumas: Negative experiences, especially during formative years, can create protective beliefs that served us once but now limit our growth. Someone who experienced public humiliation might develop the belief "It's not safe to stand out" as a way to avoid future pain, but this belief might later prevent them from pursuing leadership opportunities or sharing their gifts.

Social Comparison: In our social media saturated world, constant comparison with others can fuel beliefs about our inadequacy. "Everyone else has it figured out," "I'm behind where I should be," or "I don't have what it takes" are modern variations of ancient comparison traps.

Perfectionist Standards: High achievers often develop limiting beliefs around perfection and control. "If I can't do it perfectly, I shouldn't try at all" or "I have to figure everything out before I can start" can paralyze progress and prevent the kind of faithful risk-taking that growth requires.

The People-Pleasing Pattern: People-pleasing is a specific form of self-limiting belief rooted in the fear that our authentic selves aren't acceptable or lovable. People-pleasers unconsciously believe they must earn love and acceptance through performance rather than receiving it as a gift.

People-pleasing behaviors are often rooted in anxious attachment patterns developed early in life. When children learn that love and safety depend on meeting others' expectations rather than being authentically themselves, they develop sophisticated strategies for reading and responding to others' needs while suppressing their own.

The psychology behind people-pleasing reveals several interconnected beliefs:

- "My worth depends on others' approval"
- "Conflict is dangerous and must be avoided"
- "My needs are less important than others' needs"
- "If people really knew me, they wouldn't like me"

These beliefs drive behaviors like over-apologizing, difficulty saying no, taking responsibility for others' emotions, and chronic self-sacrifice. While these behaviors might seem generous or admirable, they often lead to resentment, burnout, and shallow relationships rather than the deep connection people-pleasers desperately seek.

Breaking Free from Self-Limiting Beliefs: The process of overcoming self-limiting beliefs begins with awareness - learning to recognize the stories you tell yourself about your capabilities and worth. This often requires "metacognition" - thinking about thinking - and the willingness to question assumptions you've held for years.

Cognitive-behavioral research provides evidence-based strategies for challenging and reframing limiting beliefs:

1. **Identify the belief**: Pay attention to your internal dialogue, especially during moments of stress or challenge. What automatic thoughts arise when you consider taking risks or pursuing goals?
2. **Examine the evidence**: What proof supports this belief? What evidence contradicts it? Often, limiting beliefs are based on outdated information or isolated incidents rather than comprehensive reality.
3. **Consider alternative perspectives**: How might a close friend view your capabilities? What would you tell someone you cared about who expressed this belief about themselves?
4. **Test the belief**: Conduct small experiments that challenge the limiting belief. If you believe you're terrible at networking, attend one professional event and practice having genuine conversations rather than trying to "work the room."
5. **Reframe the narrative**: Replace limiting beliefs with more accurate, empowering alternatives. "I'm not good at public speaking" might become "I'm developing my public speaking skills" or "I have valuable insights to share, even if I feel nervous sharing them."

Apathy and Learned Helplessness: When Hope Dies

The final category of unconscious hindrance involves *learned helplessness - a psychological state where repeated exposure to uncontrollable negative events leads to passive acceptance of difficult circumstances, even when change becomes possible.*

Seligman and Maier's (1967) original research involved dogs who were exposed to inescapable electric shocks. Initially, the dogs tried frantically to escape, but when their efforts proved futile, they eventually stopped trying. Most significantly, when these same dogs were later placed in situations where escape was possible, they remained passive, having learned that their actions didn't matter.

This phenomenon translates powerfully to human experience. When people repeatedly face situations where their efforts seem to make no difference - whether in relationships, work, health, or personal growth - they may develop a generalized sense that their actions don't matter. This learned helplessness can persist even when circumstances change and new opportunities for positive change emerge.

Common Manifestations of Learned Helplessness:

Relationship Patterns: After experiencing multiple relationship failures or betrayals, someone might stop investing emotionally in new relationships, believing that vulnerability inevitably leads to pain.

Career Stagnation: Repeated rejections, workplace disappointments, or economic setbacks can create the belief that professional advancement is beyond personal control, leading to disengagement from career development.

Health Behaviors: People who have repeatedly tried and failed to establish healthy habits might develop the belief that lasting change is impossible for them, leading to complete abandonment of health-promoting behaviors.

Spiritual Life: Christians who have experienced unanswered prayers, spiritual dryness, or church disappointments might develop learned helplessness in their relationship with God, going through spiritual motions without expecting genuine encounter or transformation.

The Neurobiology of Learned Helplessness: Neuroscience has supported the findings that learned helplessness involves specific changes in brain chemistry and structure. Chronic stress and perceived lack of control affect the prefrontal cortex (responsible for executive function and decision-making) and the hippocampus (involved in learning and memory). These changes can create a self-reinforcing cycle where helplessness becomes both the symptom and the cause of continued passivity.

Breaking the Cycle of Learned Helplessness: The antidote to learned helplessness isn't simply positive thinking or willpower, but rather what Seligman later termed "learned optimism" and "learned hopefulness". This involves:

Specific Attribution: Instead of viewing setbacks as evidence of global personal inadequacy ("I always fail"), learn to make specific attributions ("This particular strategy didn't work in this situation").

Temporary Framing: Rather than viewing problems as permanent ("I'll never be good at this"), practice seeing them as temporary challenges that can be addressed with time and effort.

External Perspective: Recognize that many factors influence outcomes beyond personal control, without using this as an excuse to avoid responsibility where it exists.

Incremental Success: Create opportunities for small wins that rebuild the sense of personal agency and effectiveness. These don't have to be dramatic - even minor positive changes can begin to rewire the brain's expectation that effort leads to results.

Community Support: *Learned helplessness is more easily overcome in supportive community contexts where others believe in your capacity for change and provide encouragement during the rebuilding process.*

The Philosophical Foundation: What Really Drives Your Decisions?

Beneath all these specific hindrances lies a deeper question that most of us rarely examine consciously: What fundamental philosophy or worldview actually guides your life choices? While we might claim to operate from Christian principles, financial pragmatism, family values, or personal fulfillment, our actual decision-making patterns often reveal competing or conflicting philosophical foundations operating unconsciously.

Competing Worldviews in Christian Life: Even committed Christians often operate from multiple, sometimes contradictory philosophical frameworks without realizing it:

- **Materialism vs. Eternal Perspective**: While affirming eternal values, daily decisions might be driven primarily by financial security, status symbols, or comfort.
- **Individual Success vs. Community Good**: Despite theological commitments to community, decisions might consistently prioritize personal advancement over collective flourishing.
- **Control vs. Trust**: While intellectually believing in God's sovereignty, behavioral patterns might reveal deep investment in maintaining personal control over outcomes.
- **Performance vs. Grace**: Though embracing the gospel of grace theologically, practical life might be driven by unconscious beliefs about earning worth through achievement and moral performance.

The Integration Challenge: The goal isn't to eliminate all competing influences - we live in a complex world that requires navigating multiple valid considerations. Rather, it's about making conscious choices about which values take precedence when different philosophical commitments conflict. This requires ongoing examination of the gap between stated beliefs and actual behaviors, pursued with grace and commitment to growth rather than harsh self-condemnation.

Practical Tools for Making the Unconscious Conscious

The process of identifying and addressing unconscious hindrances requires specific tools and practices that bring hidden patterns into the light of conscious examination.

The Hindrance Assessment Worksheet

Step 1: Pattern Recognition
For one week, keep a simple decision journal. Note significant choices you make each day and the reasoning (or lack thereof) behind them. Look for patterns:

- What decisions do you make automatically without conscious deliberation?
- When do you find yourself saying "that's just how I've always done it"?
- What areas of life feel "stuck" despite your stated desires for change?

Step 2: Generational Inventory

- What patterns from your family of origin do you see repeating in your current life?
- What messages about money, relationships, work, and faith did you receive growing up - both spoken and unspoken?
- Which inherited patterns serve you well, and which might benefit from conscious examination?

Step 3: Cultural Influence Assessment

- How do the expectations of your cultural background influence your goals and decisions?
- What cultural messages about success, gender roles, family obligations, and personal fulfillment operate in your life?
- Where do you see conflicts between cultural expectations and personal calling?

Step 4: Self-Limiting Belief Identification

- What automatic negative thoughts arise when you consider taking risks or pursuing dreams?
- Complete these sentences: "I could never..." "People like me don't..." "It's too late for me to..."
- What experiences or messages contributed to the formation of these beliefs?

Step 5: Helplessness Inventory

- What areas of your life feel completely beyond your control?
- Where have you stopped trying because previous efforts seemed ineffective?
- What would you pursue if you truly believed your efforts could make a difference?

Step 6: Philosophical Foundation Examination

- When facing difficult decisions, what factors do you actually consider first?
- What does your calendar and bank account reveal about your true priorities?
- Where do you see gaps between your stated values and your behavioral patterns?

Integration and Action Planning

Once you've identified specific hindrances, the next step is developing a plan for addressing them with wisdom and grace:

Prioritize Consciousness Over Perfection: The goal isn't to eliminate all unconscious influences - that would be impossible and unnecessary. Rather, focus on bringing awareness to patterns that most significantly limit your growth and calling.

Start Small: Choose one or two specific areas for focused attention rather than trying to overhaul everything simultaneously. *Sustainable change happens through consistent small steps rather than dramatic transformations.*

Seek Community Input: Share your discoveries with trusted friends, mentors, or counselors who can offer perspective and accountability. Others often see our patterns more clearly than we do.

Embrace Grace in the Process: Remember that uncovering unconscious patterns is often uncomfortable and sometimes painful. Approach this work with the same compassion you would offer a dear friend facing similar discoveries.

Celebrate Awareness as Victory: Simply recognizing a previously unconscious pattern is significant progress, even before you've changed the behavior. Awareness creates space for choice, which is the foundation of transformation.

Moving Forward: From Unconscious to Intentional

As we prepare to move into our next chapter on distractions, take a moment to acknowledge the courage it requires to examine the unconscious forces shaping your life. This kind of self-examination isn't comfortable, but it's essential for the kind of authentic transformation that leads to greater freedom and effectiveness in serving God and others.

The hindrances we've explored - generational patterns, cultural conditioning, self-limiting beliefs, and learned helplessness - aren't character flaws or spiritual failures. They're simply human realities that affect everyone to some degree. The difference between those who experience ongoing growth and those who remain stuck isn't the absence of these patterns but rather the willingness to examine them with honesty and address them with wisdom.

Jung's insight that unconscious forces will direct our lives until we make them conscious points to both the challenge and the hope of personal transformation. The challenge is that this work requires vulnerability, patience, and the willingness to question assumptions we may have held for years. The hope is that conscious awareness creates space for intentional choice - the ability to respond rather than merely react, to choose rather than simply follow inherited patterns.

In our next chapter, we'll explore how external distractions compete for our attention and energy, often preventing us from doing the deep work of transformation we've begun here. But for now, rest in the assurance that God sees and understands the forces that have shaped you, and He offers both grace for the journey and power for the changes that align with His purposes for your life.

Journal Prompts:

- What unconscious patterns did you recognize in yourself as you read this chapter?
- Which category of hindrances (generational, cultural, self-limiting beliefs, learned helplessness) feels most relevant to your current growth challenges?
- What inherited patterns from your family or culture do you want to examine more closely?
- What self-limiting beliefs have you been carrying that might be ready for challenge?
- In what areas of your life have you experienced learned helplessness? What small step could you take to begin rebuilding your sense of agency in one of these areas?
- How do you sense God inviting you to greater freedom through this process of making the unconscious conscious?

The journey from stuck to unstoppable requires facing these hidden barriers with courage and grace. As you continue forward, remember that every moment of awareness is a victory, every conscious choice is progress, and every step toward freedom serves not just your own flourishing but also your capacity to love and serve others more fully.

Chapter 5 Summary

📋 Key Concepts:

- 99.99% of brain processing happens unconsciously
- Generational transmission through family patterns and epigenetics
- Cultural conditioning creates invisible "water we swim in"
- Self-limiting beliefs operate as self-fulfilling prophecies
- Learned helplessness can be overcome through specific interventions

⚡ Action Items:

- Complete the Hindrance Assessment Worksheet
- Map your generational patterns (positive and negative)
- Identify cultural messages that may limit authentic growth
- Challenge three specific self-limiting beliefs with evidence
- Take one small action in an area where you've felt helpless

🎯 **Main Takeaway:** Making unconscious influences conscious creates space for intentional choice.

Step #4
Distractions

Chapter 6: Distractions - Attention Hijackers

"The successful warrior is the average man with laser-like focus." ~Bruce Lee

Picture this scene: A father kneels under a car with two young children sitting nearby, watching him work. To one child - whose world has been safe and predictable - this is simply daddy fixing something interesting. But to another child, whose life has been marked by trauma and unpredictability, this same scene triggers a cascade of anxiety. Their nervous system, trained by past experience to scan for danger, transforms an ordinary moment into a potential threat. One child sees curiosity; the other sees catastrophe waiting to happen.

This powerful illustration from Bessel van der Kolk's "The Body Keeps the Score" reveals something profound about human attention: it's not just a cognitive function - it's a survival mechanism shaped by our experiences, environment, and emotional state. And in our current digital age, this ancient system designed to keep us alive is being constantly hijacked by forces that compete relentlessly for our most precious resource: our focused attention.

Social psychology has confirmed what many of us instinctively know: attention is fundamentally limited. We simply cannot process and respond to all the information bombarding us at any given moment. Yet we live in a world specifically engineered to fracture this limited resource, pulling our focus in countless directions while demanding we remain productive, present, and purposeful. Understanding how external forces hijack our attention - and learning to reclaim it - isn't just about better time management. It's about reclaiming our capacity for the deep work of transformation that God calls us to.

The Science of Limited Attention: Why We Can't Do It All

For over a century, psychologists have understood that attention operates as a limited resource. William James, often considered the father of American psychology, wrote in 1890 that attention "implies withdrawal from some things in order to deal effectively with others". Modern neuroscience has validated this insight with stunning precision, revealing the specific neural mechanisms that create our attentional bottlenecks.

Advanced brain imaging technology shows that our prefrontal cortex - the brain's command center responsible for focus and decision-making - can only maintain concentrated attention on a limited number of items simultaneously. When we exceed this capacity, performance degrades rapidly across all tasks. This isn't a character flaw or lack of willpower - it's a fundamental constraint of human neurological architecture.

What makes this particularly relevant for personal transformation is that *attention serves multiple functions simultaneously. It's required for maintaining information in working memory, filtering out irrelevant stimuli, controlling* emotional responses, and executing complex decisions. When external distractions fragment our attention, they don't just interrupt our current task - they compromise our capacity for the kind of sustained, deliberate effort that lasting change requires.

The Myth of Multitasking: Despite popular belief, neuroscience has definitively shown that *the brain doesn't truly multitask except for highly automated activities. Instead, it performs rapid "task-switching," which creates "attention residue" - cognitive resources that remain partially engaged with the previous task even after switching to something new.*

This switching comes with significant costs. Studies show that it takes an average of 23 minutes to fully refocus on the original task after an interruption. If we're interrupted every 15 minutes - which is common in our hyperconnected world - we never actually achieve deep focus on anything. *We exist in a state of continuous partial attention that prevents the kind of sustained engagement necessary for meaningful growth and transformation.*

Environmental Forces from the Past: When Trauma Shapes Attention

Before we can address current distractions, we must understand how past experiences shape our attentional patterns. Trauma, in particular, creates lasting changes in how we scan and respond to our environment, often turning our attention into a hypervigilant surveillance system rather than a focused tool for growth.

The Hypervigilance Response

Hypervigilance is a state of heightened alertness where individuals continuously scan their environment for potential threats. Eye-tracking technology has been used to find that people experiencing hypervigilance demonstrate significantly more visual fixations across a broader area compared to those in relaxed states. They're essentially spreading their attention thin across the entire visual field rather than focusing deeply on relevant information.

This pattern, while adaptive in genuinely dangerous situations, becomes problematic when it persists in safe environments. *The constant scanning not only fragments attention but also increases autonomic arousal - elevating heart rate, blood pressure, and stress hormone levels. Over time, this creates a self-reinforcing cycle: heightened arousal increases perceived threats, which justifies more scanning, which maintains the arousal.*

The Neurological Impact: Hypervigilance involves overactivation of the amygdala (the brain's alarm system) and underactivation of the prefrontal cortex (responsible for rational decision-making and focused attention). This neurological pattern makes sustained attention on growth-oriented activities extremely difficult because the brain remains primed to interrupt focus whenever it detects potential problems - which, in a hypervigilant state, is almost constantly.

Body Posture and Attention

Fascinating work by Amy Cuddy and her colleagues revealed that even our physical posture can influence our attentional capacity and stress response. In their landmark study, participants who assumed "high-power poses" (expansive, open postures like leaning back with hands behind the head) for just two minutes showed measurable increases in testosterone and decreases in cortisol compared to those who held "low-power poses" (contractive, closed postures).

While subsequent research has raised questions about the replicability of all the original findings, the core insight remains supported: our physical presence influences our psychological state, including our capacity for focused attention. When we physically contract - hunching over devices, crossing our arms defensively, or collapsing into stressed postures - we may be inadvertently signaling to our nervous system that we're under threat, which fragments our attentional capacity.

Practical Application: The way we hold our bodies while working, studying, or engaging in personal growth activities isn't merely about comfort - it's about optimizing our neurological state for sustained attention. *Sitting or standing in open, confident postures may actually support better focus by keeping our stress response systems calm.*

The Dopamine Hijack: How Rewards Fragment Attention

Modern technology has weaponized one of our most fundamental neurological systems: the brain's reward circuitry. Understanding how this system works - and how it's being exploited - is crucial for reclaiming control over our attention.

The Neuroscience of Digital Addiction

Every notification, like, comment, or message triggers a release of dopamine in the brain's reward pathway. But dopamine isn't actually about pleasure - it's about anticipation and motivation. It's the neurochemical that makes us want to seek out potentially rewarding experiences.

Digital platforms exploit what psychologists call "intermittent variable reward schedules" - the same principle that makes slot machines addictive. We never know when we'll receive a notification (intermittent) or whether it will be something rewarding like an encouraging message or something mundane like a system update (variable). This unpredictability causes our brains to release dopamine not when we actually receive a reward, but in anticipation of potentially receiving one.

The result is a powerful craving cycle that operates below conscious awareness. Our devices become "external dopamine pumps," constantly promising reward while delivering intermittent reinforcement. This creates "wanting without liking" - a compulsive urge to check our devices even when we derive little actual satisfaction from doing so.

The Jack-of-All-Trades Syndrome

This constant promise of reward creates what we might call "jack-of-all-trades syndrome" - the tendency to scatter our attention across multiple activities because each promises its own form of immediate gratification. Instead of developing deep expertise or sustained focus in meaningful areas, we become addicted to the quick hits of accomplishment that come from jumping between tasks.

Consider how this pattern might have developed in childhood. A bright, exceptionally capable girl in third grade learns that she can get praise from her teacher by quickly completing assignments, even if she cuts corners. The immediate reward of approval becomes more compelling than the delayed satisfaction of mastery. Over time, this pattern shapes her approach to learning and growth, prioritizing speed and external validation over depth and intrinsic satisfaction.

Years later in adulthood, she might find herself constantly switching between projects, always seeking the next source of quick accomplishment rather than staying with the challenging, uncertain work of deep transformation. The problem isn't lack of capability - it's an attention system trained to seek immediate rewards rather than sustained engagement.

Current Environmental Constraints: The Attention Economy

We live in an "attention economy" - a system where human attention has become the primary currency. Technology companies employ teams of neuroscientists, behavioral economists, and user experience designers whose job is to capture and monetize our focus. Understanding this reality isn't about demonizing technology but about recognizing the scale of forces working against sustained attention.

The Distraction-by-Design Problem

Modern digital environments are specifically engineered to create what Nir Eyal calls "habit loops" that keep users engaged. Features like infinite scroll, autoplay videos, push notifications, and "streak" systems are all designed to hijack our attention by exploiting psychological vulnerabilities. These aren't accidental byproducts of technology - they're intentional design choices based on sophisticated research into human psychology.

The average smartphone user receives 80-100 notifications per day. Each notification creates what psychologists call a *"cognitive switch cost" - mental energy expended in shifting attention from the current task to the notification and back again. Even if we don't immediately respond to the notification, simply knowing it's there reduces our cognitive performance on the primary task.*

The Illusion of Balanced Life

The modern concept of "work-life balance" may itself be problematic when it comes to attention management. Trying to maintain perfect balance across multiple life domains simultaneously may actually fragment our attention and reduce effectiveness in all areas.

Instead of balance, what we may need is what Cal Newport calls "attention residue management" - the ability to fully shift our focus from one domain to another rather than trying to maintain partial attention across multiple areas simultaneously. This doesn't mean ignoring important relationships or responsibilities but rather developing the capacity to be fully present to whatever deserves our focus in any given moment.

Distractions as Anesthesia: Avoiding the Uncomfortable Work of Growth

One of the most subtle but powerful ways distractions hijack our attention is by providing escape from uncomfortable emotions or challenging growth work. Video games, social media, streaming services, shopping, and even productivity apps can become sophisticated avoidance mechanisms that prevent us from engaging with the difficult but necessary work of transformation.

The Neuroscience of Avoidance

Behavioral psychology reveals that *humans have a strong tendency to avoid activities associated with negative emotions, even when those activities would serve our long-term interests.* When we associate personal growth work with discomfort - whether that's the vulnerability of honest self-examination, the frustration of changing ingrained habits, or the uncertainty of pursuing new directions - our brains naturally seek alternatives that provide immediate relief.

Digital distractions are particularly effective at providing this relief because they offer "flow experiences" with minimal entry barriers. Unlike the demanding work of personal transformation, which requires sustained effort and tolerance for discomfort, digital entertainment provides immediate engagement with predictable rewards

Studies of behavioral addiction reveal that people often turn to distracting activities not because they find them inherently enjoyable, but because they provide temporary escape from anxiety, depression, or feelings of inadequacy. The distraction doesn't solve the underlying problem - it simply postpones the discomfort while creating additional problems through neglect of important growth work.

The Anesthesia Effect

Consider how anesthesia works in medical procedures: it blocks pain signals so that necessary but uncomfortable interventions can be performed. Digital distractions can function similarly, blocking the emotional discomfort that often accompanies meaningful change. The problem is that unlike medical anesthesia, these distractions prevent the "surgery" from taking place rather than enabling it.

Avoidance behaviors tend to increase in frequency and intensity over time. What begins as occasional escape from discomfort can evolve into compulsive patterns that consume significant time and attention. The temporary relief becomes the primary coping strategy, preventing the development of more adaptive approaches to managing difficult emotions.

The Interruption Epidemic: When We Invite Distraction

Perhaps the most troubling aspect of modern attention fragmentation is how much of it is self-imposed. A recent statistic shows that people interrupt their own work every 11-15 minutes on average, often to check email, social media, or news. We've become complicit in our own distraction, inviting interruptions even when no external forces require them.

The Open-Door Policy Problem

Many of us operate with what might be called an "open door policy" toward distractions. We leave notifications enabled, keep social media tabs open while working, and position ourselves in environments filled with potential interruptions. This reflects a misunderstanding about the nature of creative and transformative work.

Academic observations of peak performance consistently shows that meaningful accomplishment requires periods of sustained, uninterrupted focus. Yet we often treat attention like an infinitely renewable resource that can be divided without consequence. Studies reveal that *even the mere presence of a smartphone - even when turned off and face-down - can reduce cognitive performance by 10-15% because part of our mental capacity is dedicated to resisting the urge to check it.*

The Fear of Missing Out (FOMO) Driver

Much of our invitation to distraction is driven by what psychologists term FOMO - fear of missing out. Social media platforms exploit this fear by creating artificial urgency around information that is rarely truly urgent. Breaking news, friend updates, and viral content are designed to feel immediately important when they rarely require immediate attention.

The irony is that by trying to stay current with everything, we often miss what's most important. The person constantly checking news might miss the subtle emotional cues from their spouse. The individual scrolling social media might overlook opportunities for deep reflection or creative insight that arise during quiet moments.

Practical Strategies for Attention Reclamation

Understanding the forces that fragment our attention is only the beginning. The real work lies in developing practical strategies for protecting and directing this precious resource toward growth and purpose.

Environmental Design for Focus

Digital Boundaries: Creating specific boundaries around technology use is an especially effective tactic within environmental design. This might include designated phone-free zones, specific times for checking email and social media, and the use of apps that block distracting websites during focused work periods.

Physical Environment: Our physical environment sends constant signals to our attention system. Cluttered, noisy, or chaotic environments require ongoing mental energy to filter out irrelevant stimuli. Creating calm, organized spaces for growth work can significantly improve our capacity for sustained focus.

Temporal Boundaries: Protecting specific times for uninterrupted focus is crucial. This means not just scheduling time for important work but actively defending that time against interruptions. Even short periods of deep focus (45-90 minutes) can be more productive than longer periods of fragmented attention.

Attention Training Practices

Mindfulness and Meditation: Numerous studies confirm that even 10-20 minutes of daily meditation and mindfulness practice can improve sustained attention and reduce mind-wandering.

Single-tasking Practice: Deliberately practicing single-tasking - giving complete attention to one activity at a time - helps retrain our attention system. This might involve eating a meal without checking phones, having conversations without multitasking, or reading without background distractions.

Attention Restoration: Environmental psychology confirms what common sense and life experience has taught us: that certain activities naturally restore our capacity for focused attention. Time in nature, physical exercise, and creative activities that we find genuinely engaging can replenish our attentional resources.

Trauma-Informed Attention Work

For individuals whose attention patterns have been shaped by trauma or chronic stress, additional strategies may be helpful:

Nervous System Regulation: Learning techniques for calming the nervous system - such as deep breathing, progressive muscle relaxation, or gentle movement - can help shift the brain out of hypervigilant states that fragment attention.

Grounding Practices: Techniques that help individuals feel safe and present in their current environment can reduce the need for constant environmental scanning. This might include sensory grounding exercises or creating physical spaces that feel particularly safe and calming.

Professional Support: For individuals dealing with significant trauma responses that impact attention, working with a trauma-informed therapist or counselor can be crucial for developing effective coping strategies.

The Motives and Time Assessment: Making the Invisible Visible

To effectively reclaim our attention, we need to make our current patterns visible. This requires honest assessment of how we're currently using our time and attention, and what motives drive our choices.

The Attention Audit

Time Tracking: For one week, keep a detailed log of how you spend your time, particularly noting:

- When you check your phone or computer for non-essential purposes
- How long you can focus on important tasks before feeling compelled to switch
- What triggers your urges for distraction (boredom, anxiety, fatigue, etc.)
- Which activities genuinely restore your energy versus drain it

Interruption Inventory: Notice both external interruptions (notifications, other people, environmental noise) and internal interruptions (wandering thoughts, emotional reactions, physical discomfort). Understanding your personal patterns is the first step in addressing them.

Values-Attention Alignment: Compare how you spend your attention with your stated values and goals. Where do you see alignment? Where do you notice significant gaps? This isn't about judgment but about awareness that can inform better choices.

Motive Examination

Reward Seeking: What forms of immediate gratification are you using to avoid more challenging but important work? This might include social media, online shopping, news consumption, or even productive activities that serve as sophisticated procrastination.

Anxiety Management: How much of your attention fragmentation is driven by anxiety or hypervigilance? Are you unconsciously scanning for problems rather than focusing on solutions and growth?

Identity Reinforcement: Sometimes we maintain scattered attention because it reinforces our identity as busy, important, or needed. Examine whether your attention patterns serve your authentic growth or merely maintain a self-image that may no longer serve you.

Integration and Moving Forward

As we prepare to move into our next chapter on relational influences, take time to recognize the courage required to examine your attention patterns honestly. In a culture that profits from fragmented attention, choosing to focus deeply is both a personal and political act. It's a declaration that your growth, your relationships, and your calling deserve the full engagement of your mind and heart.

The research we've explored reveals that attention isn't just about productivity or efficiency - it's about the quality of our engagement with life itself. When our attention is constantly fragmented, we miss opportunities for deep connection, creative insight, and spiritual growth. We become reactive rather than responsive, scattered rather than centered.

But the same neuroplasticity that allows negative patterns to become entrenched also makes positive change possible. Every moment of focused attention strengthens the neural pathways that support sustained concentration. Every choice to engage deeply rather than surf shallow waters builds our capacity for the transformative work that awaits us.

Journal Prompts:

- What patterns of attention fragmentation did you recognize in yourself as you read this chapter?
- How might past experiences or trauma be influencing your current attention patterns?
- What specific distractions do you use to avoid uncomfortable emotions or challenging growth work?
- Where do you see the biggest gaps between how you currently use your attention and how you'd like to use it?
- What environmental changes could you make to better support sustained attention?
- How might your physical posture and presence be affecting your capacity for focus?
- What would become possible in your life if you could consistently engage in deep, sustained attention on what matters most?

The journey from stuck to unstoppable requires not just knowing what to do but developing the capacity to stay focused on doing it consistently over time. In our next chapter, we'll explore how the people around us can either support or undermine this focused engagement with growth. But for now, rest in the assurance that every step you take toward reclaiming your attention is a step toward reclaiming your life.

Your attention is one of your most precious gifts - not just to yourself, but to everyone whose lives you touch. The world needs people who can think deeply, engage fully, and respond wisely rather than merely react quickly. As you work to protect and direct this invaluable resource, you're not just serving your own growth - you're contributing to a world that desperately needs the fruits of sustained, purposeful attention.

Chapter 8 Summary

Key Concepts:

- Attention is fundamentally limited (40 bits vs. 11 million processed)
- Hypervigilance from trauma fragments attentional capacity
- Digital platforms exploit dopamine reward systems
- Multitasking is actually rapid task-switching with cognitive costs

Action Items:

- Conduct a one-week attention audit
- Create phone-free zones and times
- Practice single-tasking deliberately
- Develop transition rituals between life domains
- Address trauma-related hypervigilance if present

Main Takeaway: Reclaiming focused attention from modern distractions is essential for the sustained engagement that transformation requires.

Step #5
Weeds

Chapter 7: Weeds - Relational Influence That Chokes Growth

"The people you surround yourself with either lift you up or bring you down. There is no neutral."
~Unknown

Picture a beautifully tended garden where a gardener has carefully planted seeds according to their unique design and purpose. Each plant has the potential to flourish and produce fruit that only it can provide. But if the gardener allows weeds to take root and grow unchecked, something tragic happens: these invasive influences don't just coexist peacefully with the intended crop - they actively compete for the same soil, sunlight, and nutrients. Eventually, the weeds can grow so thick and aggressive that they choke out the very plants the garden was designed to nurture.

This is exactly what happens in the garden of our lives when we allow too many influences - or the wrong influences - to take root in our relational soil. The people, voices, opinions, and expectations that we permit to shape our daily reality don't remain neutral observers of our growth. They become active participants, either nurturing the unique calling and gifts God has planted within us, or systematically choking them out through their competing demands, contradictory messages, or toxic patterns.

What makes this particularly challenging is that not all relational influences announce themselves as weeds. A dandelion might be an invasive pest to one gardener but a valuable source of nutrition to another. Similarly, relationships that might be perfectly healthy for someone else could become growth-choking weeds in the specific soil of your life and calling. The key isn't to eliminate all social influence - that would be impossible and unwise. Instead, it's learning to discern which relational forces support your authentic growth and which threaten to subsume your unique contribution entirely.

The Science of Social Influence: How Others Shape Us

Social psychology has spent over a century documenting the profound ways that other people shape our thoughts, emotions, decisions, and behaviors. Their work reveals something both humbling and empowering: we are far more influenced by our social environment than most of us realize, but understanding these dynamics gives us the power to choose our influences more intentionally.

The Neuroscience of Social Influence: Recent advances in neuroimaging have revealed that social influence operates at the most fundamental levels of brain function. When we're exposed to others' opinions, specific neural networks activate that involve not just rational decision-making centers but also reward pathways and emotional processing regions. This means that *social influence isn't just about consciously considering others' perspectives - it's about our brains literally finding it rewarding to align with social information.*

The relatively new methodology of computational modeling has identified three core mechanisms underlying social influence: valuation (how we assess the worth of others' opinions), action selection (how we decide whether to conform or resist), and learning (how we update our beliefs based on social feedback). These processes operate continuously and largely outside our conscious awareness, meaning we're constantly being shaped by social forces whether we recognize it or not.

Individual Differences in Susceptibility: Not everyone is equally influenced by social pressure. Several factors determine how susceptible we are to social influence, including age (adolescents are generally more susceptible), personality traits (people-pleasers and those with low self-esteem are more easily influenced), social status (those with lower perceived status are more likely to conform), and cultural background (collectivistic cultures show different patterns of social influence than individualistic ones).

Importantly, statistics show that socioeconomic status also plays a crucial role. Individuals from lower socioeconomic backgrounds often show greater neural sensitivity to social exclusion and are more likely to conform to group pressure, possibly as an adaptive strategy for maintaining social support. This suggests that vulnerability to negative social influence isn't a character weakness but often reflects deeper needs for security and belonging.

Social Identity Theory: The Psychology of Belonging

To understand how relational influences can become weeds, we need to examine how group membership shapes our sense of self. Social Identity Theory, developed by Henri Tajfel and John Turner, reveals that *a significant portion of our self-concept comes not from individual characteristics but from our perceived membership in social groups.*

The Process of Social Categorization: Human beings automatically categorize themselves and others into social groups based on shared characteristics, beliefs, or affiliations. This process serves important psychological functions - it helps us make sense of complex social environments and provides a sense of belonging and identity. However, it also creates powerful in-group/out-group dynamics that can profoundly influence our behavior and decision-making.

If we pay attention, we easily recognize what researchers are telling us: once we identify with a particular group, we tend to favor in-group members, adopt group norms and values, and view our group more positively than out-groups. This process is largely unconscious and can occur even with completely arbitrary group divisions. In the famous "minimal group" experiments, people would discriminate in favor of their group members even when the groups were formed by something as trivial as a coin flip.

The Dark Side of Group Belonging: While social identity can provide valuable support and meaning, it can also become a weed that chokes out individual authenticity and calling. When group belonging becomes more important than personal integrity, when maintaining group membership requires suppressing authentic self-expression, or when group norms conflict with individual values and calling, the very relationships meant to support us can become forces that limit our growth.

Surprisingly, people will often conform to group expectations even when they privately disagree, especially when group membership is important to their self-esteem. This can create "pluralistic ignorance" - situations where everyone in a group privately questions the group's direction but assumes everyone else supports it, leading to collective decision-making that serves no one's authentic interests.

The Five-Person Limit: Managing Your Influence Circle

Dr. John Delony, a well-respected mental health expert, frequently teaches about the importance of limiting the number of people whose opinions and influence you allow to significantly impact your decisions. His work and clinical experience suggest that most people can healthily process input from no more than about five close advisors or influence sources at any given time.

The Psychological Rationale: This limit isn't arbitrary - it reflects real constraints in how our brains process social information. Evolutionary psychology suggests that human civilizations evolved from small tribal groups in which maintaining close relationships with a limited number of individuals was crucial for survival. Our neural architecture still reflects these origins, making us most effective at processing and integrating feedback from a small circle of trusted relationships rather than a large network of casual connections.

When we exceed this natural limit, several problems emerge. First, we experience "advice overload" - the cognitive fatigue that comes from trying to process too many perspectives simultaneously. Second, we become vulnerable to contradictory or conflicting input that can paralyze decision-making rather than enhance it. Third, we may begin prioritizing the maintenance of multiple relationships over authentic self-expression and growth.

The Jumanji Effect: Consider using the metaphor of the rapidly growing, consuming vines in the movie "Jumanji" to describe what happens when we allow too many influences into our inner circle. Like those fictional plants that quickly overran everything in their path, unmanaged social influences can grow so rapidly and pervasively that they completely subsume our authentic identity and calling.

This is particularly dangerous because the process often feels positive initially. Having many people who care about our decisions and want to offer input can feel supportive and validating. However, beyond a certain threshold, additional social input becomes detrimental rather than helpful. We become so focused on managing multiple relationships and expectations that we lose touch with our own values, goals, and sense of direction.

Practical Application: This doesn't mean isolating yourself or rejecting all social input. Instead, it means being intentional about whose voices you allow into your inner circle of advisors. Consider these questions:

- Whose opinions do you automatically seek when facing important decisions?
- Who has demonstrated wisdom, integrity, and genuine care for your wellbeing over time?

- Whose values align with your own deepest convictions and calling?
- Who has the capacity to offer input without becoming defensive if you choose differently?

Toxic Relationships: When Influence Becomes Poison

Not all negative relational influences are subtle or gradual. Some relationships are actively toxic, characterized by patterns that systematically undermine mental health, self-esteem, and personal growth. Understanding the psychology of toxic relationships is crucial because these dynamics can completely derail personal transformation while disguising themselves as care, concern, or love.

Defining Toxicity: This term is vastly overused today, and oftentimes by people who do not understand it. Let's consider the proper definition so we're all understanding each other. Relationship psychology defines toxic relationships as those characterized by consistent patterns of emotional manipulation, control, blame, criticism, and boundary violations. Unlike healthy relationships that involve occasional conflict or disappointment, toxic relationships create chronic stress, anxiety, and self-doubt through persistent negative patterns.

Toxic relationships often cause symptoms similar to those found in trauma survivors: hypervigilance, emotional dysregulation, difficulty trusting their own perceptions, and a persistent sense of walking on eggshells. The chronic stress of these relationships can lead to measurable changes in brain structure and function, particularly in areas responsible for decision-making and emotional regulation.

Common Toxic Patterns:

- **Gaslighting**: Deliberately distorting reality to make the victim question their own perceptions and sanity
- **Love-bombing followed by devaluation**: Intense positive attention followed by criticism and withdrawal
- **Isolation tactics**: Systematically undermining relationships with friends, family, and support networks
- **Emotional blackmail**: Using guilt, fear, or obligation to control behavior
- **Projection**: Blaming the victim for the toxic person's own behaviors and emotional responses
- **Boundary violations**: Consistently ignoring or punishing attempts to set healthy limits

The Trauma Bond: Perhaps most insidiously, toxic relationships often create what psychologists call "trauma bonds" - powerful emotional attachments that form through cycles of abuse and intermittent reinforcement. The scary reality is that *unpredictable patterns of punishment and reward create some of the strongest psychological attachments, making toxic relationships paradoxically difficult to leave even when the harm is obvious.*

This bonding pattern exploits the same neurological pathways involved in addiction, creating genuine withdrawal symptoms when the relationship is ended. *Understanding this dynamic is crucial for anyone trying to break free from toxic influences - the difficulty isn't a sign* of weakness but a predictable neurobiological response to intermittent reinforcement.

Offense and Apathy: The Emotional Weeds

Two particularly destructive emotional patterns can take root in our relational soil and choke out healthy growth: chronic offense-taking and pervasive apathy. While these might seem like opposite problems, both represent forms of emotional dysregulation that prevent us from engaging authentically and effectively with our calling and relationships.

The Psychology of Offense

Moral psychology (there sure are a lot of branches of psychology, aren't there?) shows that taking offense involves a complex interplay of violated expectations, identity threats, and social norms. When we feel offended, our brains are essentially signaling that someone has violated a rule or norm that we consider important to our identity or moral framework.

The Violated Norm Theory: This theory, developed by DeRidder and Tripathi in 1992, suggests that feeling offended specifically occurs when we perceive that someone has violated a norm we endorse, and we judge this violation to be intentional or negligent. This explains why the same behavior might be deeply offensive to one person while being completely acceptable to another - the difference lies not in the behavior itself but in the norms each person holds and how central those norms are to their identity.

When Offense Becomes a Weed: While appropriate offense can serve important social functions - signaling value violations and motivating corrective action - *chronic offense-taking becomes a relational (and spiritual!) weed that chokes out growth and connection.* People who are easily offended often struggle with:

- Rigid thinking patterns that leave little room for complexity or nuance
- High sensitivity to perceived threats to their identity or worldview
- Difficulty maintaining relationships due to frequent conflict
- Tendency to focus more energy on what others are doing wrong than on their own growth and calling

Chronic offense often reflects underlying insecurity about one's own values or identity. When our sense of self is fragile or uncertain, we may become hypervigilant about protecting it from any perceived challenge or violation.

The Problem of Apathy

On the opposite end of the spectrum, apathy - a persistent lack of motivation, interest, or emotional engagement - can also function as a relational weed that prevents authentic growth and connection. Apathy involves dysfunction in multiple domains: behavioral activation, social motivation, and emotional sensitivity.

The Neuroscience of Apathy: Apathy involves disruption in the brain networks that are responsible for goal-directed behavior, particularly the prefrontal cortex-basal ganglia circuits. This isn't simply laziness or lack of willpower - it's a genuine neurobiological state that can be triggered by chronic stress, depression, or repeated experiences of helplessness.

Apathy as Protective Withdrawal: In relational contexts, apathy often develops as a protective response to repeated disappointment, betrayal, or overwhelm. When previous attempts at engagement have resulted in pain or exhaustion, the brain may essentially "shut down" emotional investment as a way of preventing further harm.

However, while this protective withdrawal might provide temporary relief, it also prevents the kind of engaged relationship and purposeful action necessary for personal growth and meaningful contribution. *Apathy is associated with poorer life outcomes across multiple domains: relationships, career achievement, physical health, and overall life satisfaction.*

Breaking the Apathy Cycle: Overcoming apathy requires carefully titrated re-engagement that rebuilds confidence in one's ability to effect positive change. This often means starting with very small, manageable goals and gradually increasing investment as success experiences accumulate.

Identifying Your Unique Crop: What Only You Can Provide

The metaphor of weeds versus crops implies something crucial: there is a specific harvest that your life is meant to produce - a unique contribution that only you can make to the world. *Authentic self-expression and the pursuit of personally meaningful goals are among the strongest predictors of life satisfaction and psychological wellbeing.*

The Concept of Signature Strengths: Positive psychology has identified "signature strengths" - the specific combination of talents, values, and motivations that create each person's unique capacity for contribution. These aren't just things you're good at, but activities and contributions that energize rather than drain you, that feel authentic rather than forced, and that create value for others while fulfilling your own sense of purpose.

Your unique crop represents the intersection of several factors:

- **Natural talents and abilities**: The things that come relatively easily to you and that you can develop without excessive struggle
- **Deep values and convictions**: The principles that you're willing to sacrifice for and that remain consistent across different life circumstances
- **Life experiences and perspective**: The unique combination of challenges, opportunities, and insights that only you possess
- **Calling and purpose**: The sense of mission or contribution that gives your life meaning and direction
- **Service opportunities**: The specific ways that your unique combination of gifts, experiences, and values can meet genuine needs in the world

The Integration Challenge: The goal isn't to identify these elements in isolation but to understand how they work together to create your distinctive contribution. This is what Doc Pratt modeled so beautifully - he understood that his medical expertise, servant's heart, teaching gifts, and playful personality weren't separate aspects of his identity but integrated elements of his unique calling to heal, teach, and encourage others.

Protecting Your Crop: Boundary Setting and Influence Management

Once you've identified the unique contribution you're called to make, the next challenge is creating relational and environmental conditions that support rather than undermine this calling. This requires "boundary management" - the ability to protect your time, energy, and emotional resources so they can be directed toward your highest priorities.

The Science of Boundaries: Maintaining clear, healthy boundaries is imperative for achieving higher levels of life satisfaction, better mental health, and more authentic relationships. *Boundaries aren't walls that separate us from others - they're more like the cellular membranes that allow healthy exchange while preventing toxic substances from entering and essential resources from leaking out.*

Boundary-setting activates specific brain networks associated with self-regulation and executive function. *People who regularly practice boundary-setting show increased activity in prefrontal cortex regions responsible for decision-making and emotional regulation, suggesting that this skill literally strengthens our capacity for intentional living.*

Types of Relational Boundaries:

- **Time boundaries**: Protecting specific periods for important work, rest, and relationship
- **Emotional boundaries**: Choosing how much emotional energy to invest in others' problems and decisions
- **Physical boundaries**: Managing access to your personal space and physical presence
- **Information boundaries**: Limiting exposure to negative news, gossip, or information overload
- **Value boundaries**: Refusing to compromise core convictions for social acceptance or approval

The Boundary Paradox: Here's an important paradox about boundaries: people with the clearest, most consistent boundaries often have the healthiest, most intimate relationships. This occurs because boundaries create safety and predictability that allow for deeper trust and vulnerability. When people know what to expect from us and trust that we'll honor our commitments, they can engage more authentically rather than walking on eggshells or testing limits.

The Worksheet: Assessing Your Relational Garden

To apply these insights practically, you need to conduct an honest assessment of the relational influences currently operating in your life. This isn't about judgment or condemnation - it's about clear-eyed evaluation that enables intentional choice.

Current Influence Inventory

Step 1: Map Your Influence Circle
List the people whose opinions, expectations, or approval

significantly impact your decisions. Include family members, friends, colleagues, mentors, social media connections, and even public figures whose content you regularly consume. Don't limit this to positive influences - include anyone whose disapproval would genuinely affect your choices.

Step 2: Categorize the Influences
For each person on your list, honestly assess:

- Do they generally support your authentic growth and calling, or do they pressure you toward their own agenda?
- Do they encourage your unique gifts and contributions, or do they want you to conform to their expectations?
- Do they offer wisdom and perspective, or primarily criticism and control?
- Do interactions with them generally leave you energized and inspired, or drained and discouraged?
- Do they respect your boundaries and decisions, or persistently try to override them?

Step 3: Identify the Weeds
Which relationships or influences consistently:

- Undermine your confidence in your calling and gifts?
- Create pressure to compromise your values or authentic self-expression?
- Generate chronic stress, anxiety, or self-doubt?
- Consume disproportionate amounts of time and emotional energy?
- Prevent you from pursuing growth opportunities or meaningful goals?

Crop Definition Exercise

Step 4: Clarify Your Unique Contribution
Based on your work in previous chapters, write a clear description of:

- What unique combination of gifts, experiences, and values do you bring to the world?
- What specific contribution are you called to make that only you can provide?
- What does thriving look like for you across The Six Dimensions of Health & Wellness?
- How do you want to use your influence to serve others and glorify God?

Step 5: Assess Alignment
Review your influence inventory in light of your unique calling:

- Which relationships actively support and encourage your authentic contribution?
- Which relationships are neutral - not particularly helpful but not harmful?
- Which relationships actively compete with or undermine your calling?
- What changes need to be made to better protect and nurture your unique growth?

Action Planning

Step 6: Develop Your Garden Management Plan

- Which toxic relationships need to be ended or significantly modified?

- Which neutral relationships might need clearer boundaries or reduced influence?
- Which supportive relationships deserve more investment and cultivation?
- What new relationships or influences might you need to actively seek?
- How will you protect time and energy for your unique contribution?

Integration and Moving Forward

As we prepare to move into our next chapter on the stones that trip us up, take time to acknowledge the courage required to honestly assess your relational influences. In a culture that often prioritizes social harmony over individual authenticity, choosing to protect your unique calling from competing influences is both brave and necessary.

The research we've explored reveals that we are profoundly social beings, shaped in countless ways by the people around us. This isn't a weakness - it's part of how we're designed to grow, learn, and contribute within community. The challenge is ensuring that our social influences support rather than subvert the unique contribution we're called to make.

Remember that managing relational influences isn't about becoming isolated or rejecting all input from others. It's about becoming more intentional and discerning about whose voices you allow to shape your decisions and direction. Just as a wise gardener doesn't reject all plants but carefully chooses which ones to cultivate based on the desired harvest, you can appreciate the value of many relationships while being selective about which ones you allow to influence your core identity and calling.

The goal is not perfection but progress - learning to recognize weeds more quickly, set boundaries more clearly, and invest your relational energy in connections that support your authentic growth and calling. Every step you take toward healthier relational boundaries creates more space for your unique gifts to flourish and serve others.

Journal Prompts:

- What relational patterns did you recognize in yourself as you read this chapter?
- Which relationships in your life consistently support your authentic growth, and which tend to undermine it?
- How has people-pleasing or fear of disappointing others influenced your major life decisions?
- What unique contribution are you called to make that only you can provide?
- Which boundaries do you need to establish or strengthen to better protect your calling?
- How might limiting your influence circle to about five trusted advisors change your decision-making process?
- What would it look like for you to use your own influence more intentionally to support others' authentic growth?

In our next chapter, we'll explore the setbacks and failures that can feel like insurmountable obstacles but actually provide opportunities for deeper growth and resilience. But for now, rest in the assurance that God has planted something unique and valuable within you, and He provides both the wisdom and strength necessary to protect and nurture it to full fruition.

Your life is meant to produce a harvest that only you can provide. The better you become at recognizing and removing the relational weeds that compete for your soil, sunlight, and nutrients, the more abundantly your authentic calling can flourish for the blessing of others and the glory of God.

Chapter 7 Summary

🗒 Key Concepts:

- Social influence operates through neurobiological reward pathways
- John Delony's five-person influence limit
- Apathy versus offense
- Character and shared values matter more than credentials
- Toxic relationships can create trauma-bond patterns
- Developing your own individual crop

⚡ Action Items:

- Map your current influence circle
- Limit primary influencers to five trusted people
- Identify and address toxic relationships
- Cultivate each type of supportive relationship
- Define your unique "crop" (contribution only you can make)

🎯 **Main Takeaway:** The people you allow to influence you will either nurture your unique calling or choke it out - choose your relational garden wisely.

Step #6
Stones

Chapter 8: Stones That Trip Us Up

"The greatest glory in living lies not in never falling, but in rising every time we fall."
~Nelson Mandela

Every journey toward transformation is littered with stones - some small pebbles that cause minor stumbles, others massive boulders that seem to block the path entirely. What makes these obstacles particularly challenging isn't just their presence, but their origin. Some stones were dropped on our path by others, creating barriers we never chose to face. Others we've carefully collected and carried ourselves, polishing them with repeated attention until they become monuments to our past achievements or failures. Still others we've dropped carelessly in our wake, creating stumbling blocks for those who follow.

The fascinating truth about stones, however, is that they can serve multiple purposes depending on how we approach them. The same stone that trips us up today can become a stepping stone tomorrow, or a building block for something beautiful and useful. Our response to obstacles - not the obstacles themselves - ultimately determines whether they become permanent barriers or temporary challenges that strengthen us for the journey ahead.

Understanding the psychology of setbacks, failures, and obstacles isn't about avoiding them entirely - that would be impossible and unwise. Instead, it's about developing the skills to navigate them with grace, learning, and growth. It's about recognizing when we need to remove stones from our path, when we need to climb over them, and when we need to go back and clean up the mess we've left for others.

The Science of Resilience: How We Respond to Setbacks

The field of positive psychology has revolutionized our understanding of how people respond to failure, trauma, and obstacles. The landmark work of Martin Seligman and others reveals that resilience isn't a fixed trait that some people have and others lack - it's a set of learnable skills and perspectives that can be developed over time.

Defining Resilience: Resilience is the ability to maintain or regain psychological well-being in the face of adversity. This involves both resistance (not being significantly impacted by negative events) and recovery (bouncing back relatively quickly from setbacks). Resilient individuals don't necessarily experience fewer negative emotions when facing obstacles - rather, they develop more effective strategies for managing those emotions and extracting learning from difficult experiences.

The Resilience Factors: A comprehensive systematic review identified several key factors that consistently predict resilience in the face of failure:

- **Higher self-esteem**: People with stable, positive self-regard are less likely to interpret setbacks as evidence of fundamental inadequacy
- **Positive attributional style**: The tendency to view failures as specific (not global), temporary (not permanent), and external (not entirely due to personal shortcomings)
- **Lower perfectionism**: Particularly "socially prescribed perfectionism" - the belief that others expect perfection from us
- **Emotional intelligence**: The ability to recognize, understand, and regulate emotions effectively during stressful situations
- **Growth mindset**: The belief that abilities can be developed through effort and learning

The Overconfidence Bias: Interestingly, recent statistics have revealed that people tend to systematically overestimate their own resilience and that of others. A large-scale study found that *individuals consistently overpredict the likelihood of success following failure, which can actually reduce their willingness to help others who are struggling because they assume people will "bounce back" on their own.* This finding suggests that while optimism can be helpful, unrealistic expectations about resilience can prevent us from seeking or offering the support that's actually needed for recovery.

Stones Dropped by Others: External Obstacles and Their Impact

Some of the most challenging obstacles we face were never our choice to carry. These are the stones dropped on our path by others - sometimes intentionally, sometimes carelessly, but always with lasting impact on our journey.

Prophetic Words That Wound

In religious contexts, prophetic words - statements believed to carry divine insight or direction - can profoundly impact individuals' self-perception and life trajectory. While these words are often intended to encourage and guide, they can also become psychological obstacles when they're inaccurate, manipulative, or delivered without proper care.

The Psychology of Prophetic Impact: Words delivered with spiritual authority carry disproportionate psychological weight. When someone receives a "prophetic word" about their calling, relationships, or future, their brain processes this information differently than regular advice or opinion. The perceived divine origin gives these words what psychologists call "heightened credibility," making them more likely to influence self-concept and decision-making.

When Prophecy Becomes Limitation: Inaccurate or manipulative prophetic words can create significant psychological distress. Can you relate to life as a college student on a Christian campus? I certainly can! How many times did I overhear something like, "God told me I'm supposed to marry you" or "God told me you are supposed to be a missionary to Ethiopia"? In unfortunate cases, individuals take this so-called prophecy to heart without weighing it in prayer, and restructure their entire lives around false expectations, leading to disappointment, confusion, and spiritual trauma when the predicted outcomes don't materialize. Some people become trapped by limiting prophetic words about their abilities, calling, or worth, carrying these stones for decades without questioning their accuracy.

Let's always remember the importance to weigh what others instruct us to do; Scripture repeatedly teaches to test all things (1 Thess 5:20-21, 1 Cor 14:29, 1 John 4:1-3, and more). Not only should we weigh these well-intentioned encouragements from others, but we should also be willing and able to gratefully, gracefully, and lovingly either accept or reject their statements after weighing them before God. Sometimes their message matches what we know to be true, and sometimes not.

We do not need to hear from God *only* through other people; the veil was torn! As I have personally experienced a multitude of times, and as Scripture teaches us, God speaks directly to us to give us wisdom and direction for the path and calling He has given us. Some Scripture that shows these truths are found in Matthew 27:50-51, Mark 15:38, Luke 23:45, Hebrews 10:19-20, James 1:5, Proverbs 3:5-6, Psalm 32:8, and many other places.

If this is a new idea to you, that God can so intimately interact with us, these Scriptures will give you a head start. If you want or need to discuss this further, I would love to talk with you. Message me through DocPrattMinistries.org, and we can discover together just how much God loves us and wants to be involved in our daily lives.

Back to the subject of Stones That Trip Us Up …

The Authority Problem: Prophetic words are particularly impactful when delivered by individuals in positions of spiritual authority. The combination of perceived divine insight and human authority creates a powerful influence dynamic that can be difficult for recipients to evaluate critically, especially when they're in vulnerable states seeking guidance or affirmation.

Social Trauma and Attachment Disruption

Social experiences - particularly those involving betrayal, rejection, or abuse by trusted figures - can create lasting obstacles to healthy relationships and self-development. These are some of the potential generational effects:

Attachment Trauma: Traumatic experiences, especially those occurring in close relationships, can fundamentally alter attachment styles - the basic patterns of how we connect with and trust others. Individuals who experience betrayal, abandonment, or abuse often develop "insecure attachment" patterns characterized by either anxious clinging or avoidant withdrawal in relationships.

The neurobiological impact is significant: trauma affects brain development and function, particularly in areas responsible for emotional regulation, threat detection, and social connection. Attachment trauma shows up as heightened activity in the amygdala (fear center) and reduced activity in the prefrontal cortex (rational decision-making) when facing social situations.

Intergenerational Transmission: Attachment trauma doesn't stop with the individual who experienced it directly - it can be passed down through generations via parenting patterns, family dynamics, and even epigenetic changes. Children of trauma survivors often inherit not just the stories of trauma but also the protective strategies and relational patterns developed in response to it, even when the original threat no longer exists.

Post-Traumatic Stress and Relationships: For quite obvious reasons, individuals with trauma histories, particularly those involving interpersonal betrayal, demonstrate increased difficulty with trust, intimacy, and emotional regulation in relationships. This creates ongoing obstacles to the kind of authentic connection necessary for personal growth and community support.

Manipulative Authority and Control

Authority figures' psychological manipulation can create lasting obstacles through the abuse of power and trust.

The Psychology of Manipulation: "Psychological manipulation" is defined as the deliberate use of tactics to influence and control others' thoughts, emotions, and behaviors for personal gain. Common tactics include gaslighting (making victims question their own perceptions), emotional blackmail (using guilt or fear to control behavior), and coercion (using threats or intimidation to compel compliance).

Authority-Based Manipulation: Manipulation is particularly damaging when it comes from authority figures - parents, teachers, religious leaders, or supervisors - because these relationships involve inherent power imbalances and often represent primary sources of validation and security. When authority figures abuse their position, victims often internalize the manipulation as truth about their worth, capabilities, or reality.

Long-Term Consequences: Experiences of manipulation by authority figures often develop persistent difficulties with self-trust, decision-making, and boundary-setting. They may struggle to distinguish between legitimate guidance and manipulative control, leading to either excessive compliance or defensive rebellion in future relationships.

Mile Markers That Trap Us: When Achievements Become Obstacles

Not all stones that trip us up are dropped by others. Some we create ourselves by turning normal life experiences - age, education, achievements - into rigid markers that define what's possible or appropriate for us.

The Tyranny of Age Expectations

Sometimes, age-related stereotypes and expectations can become significant obstacles to continued growth and contribution.

Ageism as Psychological Barrier: Ageism - discrimination based on age - operates through three main mechanisms: stereotypes (assumptions about what older people can or should do), prejudice (negative feelings toward age groups), and discrimination (differential treatment based on age). These forces can create internal and external obstacles to pursuing new goals, relationships, or challenges.

Internalized Age Limits: People often internalize age-related expectations, creating self-imposed limitations on what they pursue or attempt. Phrases like "I'm too old for that" or "At my age, I should..." reflect internalized ageism that can prevent individuals from pursuing calling and growth throughout their lifespan.

The Arbitrary Nature of Age Markers: Cross-cultural investigation into this subject shows that expectations about age-appropriate behavior vary dramatically across cultures and historical periods, revealing their largely arbitrary nature. What one culture considers "too old" for certain activities, another embraces as normal or even expected.

Counter-Research on Late-Life Development: *Positive psychology evidence consistently shows that cognitive abilities, creativity, and capacity for growth can continue developing well into advanced age,* making chronological age a poor predictor of actual capability, motivation, or potential for contribution.

Educational Credentials as Identity

The relationship between formal education and personal worth can become a significant obstacle to growth and authentic self-expression, operating in two primary ways:

Credential Inflation: Educational credentials have become increasingly important for social status and self-worth, sometimes beyond their actual relevance to competence or contribution. This "credential inflation" can create barriers for individuals who lack formal education but possess significant wisdom, experience, or natural ability.

Imposter Syndrome in Highly Educated: Paradoxically, highly educated individuals often struggle with imposter syndrome - feeling like frauds despite their credentials. The more advanced degrees someone holds, the more they may feel pressure to always appear knowledgeable and competent, creating obstacles to admitting ignorance, asking for help, or learning in areas outside their expertise.

The Learning Trap: Both scenarios, credential inflation and imposter syndrome, can create obstacles to continued learning. Those without formal credentials may feel inadequate to pursue new knowledge, while those with extensive credentials may feel pressure to maintain an image of expertise that prevents authentic curiosity and growth.

Achievement Addiction: When Success Becomes a Stumbling Block

The very successes that should energize us for continued growth can instead become obstacles that trap us in past accomplishments. Having achieved the long-sought-after, hard-worked-for accomplishment, we need to be wary of getting stuck in a pattern of polishing and admiring that trophy for too long. Enjoy the success and promptly use it to propel yourself forward!

The Neuroscience of Achievement Motivation

Motivation toward achievement activates specific reward pathways in the brain, creating genuine neurochemical addiction to accomplishment. This can lead to "hedonic adaptation" - the tendency for the positive emotions associated with achievement to fade quickly, requiring ever-greater accomplishments to maintain the same level of satisfaction.

The Achievement Paradox: Interestingly, people with chronically high achievement motivation often experience what seems paradoxical: success can become a barrier to further growth. Once someone achieves recognition or accomplishment in one area, they may become so invested in maintaining that identity that they avoid risks or challenges that could threaten their established reputation.

Performance vs. Mastery Goals: Studies distinguish between performance goals (focused on demonstrating ability and gaining recognition) and mastery goals (focused on learning and improvement). Individuals oriented toward performance goals may become trapped by their achievements because pursuing new challenges risks failure that could threaten their established competence image.

The "Has-Been" Syndrome

Academic observations of career development and life transitions have revealed how past achievements can become psychological obstacles to present engagement and future growth.

Living in Past Glory: "Glory days syndrome" - the tendency to repeatedly reference past successes while struggling to engage meaningfully with present opportunities - is exhibited by those individuals who derive their primary identity from past achievements. This pattern can prevent the kind of present-focused effort necessary for continued contribution and growth.

Identity Foreclosure: Developmental psychology reveals that premature commitment to an identity based on early achievements can prevent continued exploration and growth. When someone becomes "the athlete," "the scholar," or "the successful entrepreneur," they may struggle to develop other aspects of their identity or pursue new directions that don't align with their established image.

The Momentum Challenge: Maintaining forward momentum requires ongoing challenge and growth. When individuals rest too long on past achievements without pursuing new goals, they often experience decreased motivation, purpose, and life satisfaction - essentially becoming trapped by their own success.

Stones We've Dropped: Taking Responsibility for Our Impact

Perhaps the most challenging category of stones involves those we've dropped on others' paths through our words, actions, or failures. Studies within the moral psychology and interpersonal relationships fields consistently reveal the profound impact our behavior can have on others' growth and well-being.

The Psychology of Harm and Repair

Studies on interpersonal harm reveal several key insights about how our actions can create obstacles for others and what's required for meaningful repair.

Unintended Consequences: Truly, much of the harm we cause others is unintentional, arising from our own pain, limitations, or blindness rather than deliberate cruelty. However, the impact on recipients is the same regardless of intent, and taking responsibility requires acknowledging the actual effect rather than defending our intentions.

The Ripple Effect: This interpersonal harm often creates ripple effects that extend far beyond the immediate victim. When we wound someone through our words or actions, we may inadvertently affect their capacity to trust, love, and contribute in other relationships, essentially creating obstacles in multiple life areas.

Repair Requirements: Effective interpersonal healing typically requires several elements: acknowledgment of harm caused, genuine remorse, changed behavior, and often some form of restitution. Simply apologizing without understanding the impact or changing patterns is rarely sufficient for meaningful healing.

Common Ways We Drop Stones

Critical Words: The impact of criticism – harsh, shaming, or dismissive words – can create lasting obstacles to self-confidence and risk-taking. Studies show that children who receive frequent criticism often develop perfectionistic tendencies and fear of failure that persist into adulthood.

As a side note here, this is one of the main components to my social psychology doctoral research. The impact that critical words have on the neurodivergent population has vast, life-altering effect on the individual's unique potential, life calling, ability to thrive, and overall life satisfaction. Take a moment to think about the opportunities we all have on a nearly daily basis to either affirm or criticize others in our thoughts and actions. The neurodivergent individuals I'm studying are not the only ones who must navigate criticism well; we must consistently remember to view others as carefully crafted and loved by our Creator and treat them as such.

Broken Promises: Broken promises create significant obstacles to future relationship and personal development. When we fail to keep our word - whether in small matters or large - we may create lasting barriers to others' willingness to trust, depend on others, or take relational risks.

Emotional Unavailability: Our failure to be emotionally present and responsive can create significant obstacles for others' emotional growth and security. This is particularly impactful in parent-child relationships but extends to all significant relationships where others depend on our care and attention. If this is something you are currently struggling with, remember the flight attendant's wisdom of putting our own oxygen masks on first before taking care of others. The only way we can effectively be emotionally present and responsive is if we have tended to our own needs first. Mind you, this is not to be taken as an excuse to be consistently self-indulgent; this is a simply a necessity to being emotionally available and truly serve others as Doc Pratt would have.

Abuse of Authority: When we misuse positions of power or influence - whether as parents, teachers, supervisors, or spiritual leaders - we can create profound obstacles to others' development, self-trust, and future willingness to engage with authority.

The Restoration Process: Turning Stones into Stepping Stones

The goal isn't to eliminate all obstacles from life - that would be impossible and would actually hinder growth. Instead, employ specific approaches that can transform obstacles into opportunities for increased resilience, wisdom, and contribution.

Personal Transformation of Obstacles

Reframing Perspective: The way in which we choose to interpret obstacles significantly impacts their effect on our well-being and growth. Individuals who learn to view setbacks as opportunities for learning and growth rather than evidence of inadequacy show greater resilience and continued motivation.

Post-Traumatic Growth: Many individuals actually experience positive growth following traumatic or difficult experiences, developing increased appreciation for life, deeper relationships, enhanced personal strength, and clearer life priorities. This growth doesn't minimize the pain of the original experience but demonstrates that obstacles can become catalysts for positive change. I have experienced this myself and have learned whatever comes my way, it has the potential to make positive change in me.

Meaning-Making: Finding meaning and purpose in one's obstacles - whether through service to others, personal growth, or spiritual development - grants greater resilience and life satisfaction.

Cleaning Up Our Mess

Honest Assessment: The first step in addressing harm we've caused is honest assessment of our impact on others. This requires moving beyond defensiveness or minimization to genuinely understand how our actions affected others' lives and growth.

Direct Repair: Direct conversation with those we've harmed - when possible and appropriate - is often the most effective form of repair. This involves acknowledging specific harm, expressing genuine remorse, and asking what would be helpful for healing.

Indirect Repair: When direct repair isn't possible - due to death, distance, or other barriers, we can still contribute to healing by changing our behavior with others and using our experience to prevent similar harm in the future.

Community Service: Engaging in service to others, particularly in areas related to the harm we've caused, can be a meaningful form of repair that contributes to both personal healing and community benefit.

Integration and Moving Forward

As we prepare to move into our next chapter on habits and rhythms for sustained growth, take time to acknowledge both the stones that have shaped your journey and your power to determine their ongoing impact.

The research we've explored reveals that obstacles are inevitable parts of human experience, but our response to them is not predetermined. Every stone on your path - whether dropped by others, collected by yourself, or carelessly left in others' way - represents an opportunity for growth, healing, and contribution.

Remember that transformation isn't about achieving a life free from obstacles but about developing the skills, perspectives, and relationships that enable us to navigate challenges with grace and purpose. The stones that once threatened to trip you up can become the very building blocks for a life of greater resilience, wisdom, and service to others.

Journal Prompts:

- What stones dropped by others have had the most significant impact on your life journey? How have these obstacles shaped your growth, both positively and negatively?
- In what ways have age expectations, educational credentials, or past achievements become limiting factors in your current growth and decision-making?
- What stones have you dropped on others' paths through your words, actions, or failures? What repair work might be needed?
- How might reframing your current obstacles as opportunities for growth change your approach to present challenges?
- What would it look like to use your experience with obstacles to help others navigate similar challenges?
- How do you sense God inviting you to transform the stones in your life into stepping stones for greater service and impact?

In our next chapter, we'll explore how to establish the habits and rhythms that support long-term growth and resilience, creating sustainable patterns that help us navigate obstacles with increasing skill and grace. But for now, rest in the assurance that every obstacle you've faced has contributed to your unique capacity to serve others and that God can use even the most painful stones to build something beautiful and lasting.

Your journey forward doesn't require removing every stone from your path - it requires developing the strength, wisdom, and community support to walk confidently over whatever obstacles remain, while being careful not to drop stones that might hinder others who follow behind you.

Chapter 8 Summary

Key Concepts:

- Resilience factors: self-esteem, positive attribution, emotional intelligence
- Stones dropped by others: prophetic words, trauma, manipulative authority
- Mile markers as traps: age expectations, educational credentials
- Achievement addiction and "has-been" syndrome
- Taking responsibility for stones we've dropped on others

Action Items:

- Identify stones others have dropped on your path
- Challenge age-related and credential-based limitations
- Assess how past achievements may be limiting current growth
- List people you may have harmed and consider repair steps
- Reframe current obstacles as potential stepping stones

Main Takeaway: Every obstacle can become either a permanent barrier or a building block for greater resilience and wisdom, depending on your response.

Step #7 Habits & Rhythms

Chapter 9: Habits & Rhythms for The Long Game - Planting & Sustaining

"We are what we repeatedly do. Excellence, then, is not an act, but a habit." ~Aristotle

Imagine you're preparing for a journey across an uncharted territory - not a weekend getaway or a business trip, but a lifelong expedition toward becoming the person God created you to be. This isn't about reaching a destination and checking it off your list; it's about sustaining forward movement across decades, through seasons of abundance and scarcity, energy and exhaustion, clarity and confusion. For such a journey, you need more than good intentions and motivational quotes. You need a well-stocked chuck wagon filled with provisions for now, tools for the work ahead, and seeds for planting along the way.

This is the essence of developing sustainable habits and rhythms for personal transformation. Lasting change doesn't happen through dramatic overhauls or burst of intense effort, but through consistent, small actions repeated over time until they become automatic. The neuroscience is clear: our brains are literally rewired by repetitive behaviors, creating neural pathways that make certain actions easier and more natural over time.

But here's what makes this particularly challenging in our current cultural moment: we live in a world designed for speed, not sustainability. Everything promises instant results - rapid weight loss, quick career advancement, immediate emotional relief. The most profound and lasting transformations occur through "habit stacking" and "environmental design" - creating sustainable systems that support long-term growth rather than relying on willpower alone.

The Science of Lifelong Learning: Sustaining Growth Until You Reach Your Horizon

Developmental psychology research reveals something profound about human capacity: we remain capable of significant growth, learning, and transformation throughout our entire lifespan. This isn't just encouraging news - it's empirically supported evidence that challenges cultural assumptions about aging, capability, and potential.

The Neuroscience of Lifelong Learning: The adult brain maintains "neuroplasticity" - the ability to form new neural connections and pathways - throughout life. This means that the 70-year-old can literally develop new cognitive abilities, the 50-year-old can master entirely new skills, and the 40-year-old can reshape fundamental thought patterns in ways that were previously thought impossible.

A comprehensive study of adults aged 65 and above revealed that attitudes toward lifelong learning are positively associated with quality of life, while participation in learning activities correlates with improved wellbeing across multiple dimensions.

Three key components of learning that improves wellbeing throughout life: formal education (structured learning environments), informal learning (self-directed exploration), and experiential learning (growth through life experiences).

The Psychological Benefits of Sustained Learning: *Maintain learning orientations throughout life consistently correlates with higher levels of life satisfaction, better cognitive function, and increased resilience in the face of challenges.* This occurs because learning activates "intrinsic motivation" - the internal drive for growth and mastery that provides sustainable energy for long-term development.

Lifelong learners develop "learning agility" - the ability to rapidly acquire new skills and adapt to changing circumstances. This capacity becomes increasingly valuable in our rapidly changing world, where career paths, technology, and social expectations evolve continuously throughout a person's lifetime.

Practical Application for Sustainable Growth: Several strategies are effective for maintaining learning orientation across decades:

- **Curiosity Cultivation**: Regularly asking questions, exploring new ideas, and maintaining openness to different perspectives achieves better cognitive aging and higher life satisfaction.
- **Challenge Seeking**: Individuals who continuously seek appropriate levels of challenge - difficult enough to require growth but not so overwhelming

as to cause anxiety - maintain higher motivation and cognitive function over time.
- **Cross-Domain Learning**: Learning in multiple areas simultaneously (combining physical, intellectual, and creative challenges) produces synergistic effects that enhance overall cognitive health and life satisfaction.

The Rhythm of Self-Awareness: Using This Book's Framework Repeatedly

Self-awareness isn't a destination you reach and then maintain effortlessly; it is actually a dynamic process that requires ongoing attention and refinement throughout life. *As we grow, change, and encounter new circumstances, our understanding of ourselves must evolve accordingly.*

The Maintenance Model of Self-Awareness: Self-awareness operates more like physical fitness than like learned information. Just as physical strength requires regular exercise to maintain, self-awareness requires consistent practice and attention to remain accurate and useful. People who assume they "know themselves" and stop engaging in reflective practices often discover that their self-understanding has become outdated or incomplete.

Research identifies *three core components* of sustainable self-awareness that align perfectly with the framework we've been developing throughout this book:

Awareness: The ongoing ability to notice and accurately identify thoughts, emotions, motivations, and behavioral patterns as they occur.

Acceptance: The capacity to acknowledge aspects of yourself without immediately moving to judgment or change, creating space for honest assessment.

Alignment: The process of ensuring that your actions and choices remain consistent with your deepest values and authentic calling.

The Cyclical Nature of Growth: Personal development occurs in predictable cycles rather than linear progression. Individuals typically move through periods of stability, challenge, growth, and integration before encountering new areas requiring development. *This cyclical pattern means that the framework we've explored - beginning within, building solid footing, addressing hindrances, managing distractions, dealing with weeds and stones - requires repeated application at different life stages and in different contexts.*

People who revisit fundamental questions about identity, values, and purpose at regular intervals demonstrate greater life satisfaction and more authentic decision-making than those who assume their self-understanding is fixed. This suggests that *the assessment tools and reflective exercises throughout this book should be treated as ongoing practices rather than one-time activities.*

Creating a Rhythm of Self-Reflection: Specific practices for maintaining self-awareness over time are:

- **Regular Check-ins**: Conducting monthly or quarterly self-assessments supports a more accurate self-awareness than those who only reflect during crises.

- **Feedback Integration**: Regularly seeking and incorporating feedback from trusted others develops more complete and accurate self-understanding.
- **Pattern Recognition**: Tracking behavioral and emotional patterns over time helps identify subtle changes that might otherwise go unnoticed.
- **Values Clarification**: Regularly revisiting and refining your core values ensures that your growth remains aligned with your authentic self rather than external expectations.

The Rhythm of Balanced Living: Integration Across Life Domains

Research on work-life balance and psychological wellbeing reveals something crucial about sustainable growth: attempting to excel in all areas of life simultaneously often leads to burnout and fragmentation, while neglecting important domains creates instability that ultimately undermines progress in other areas.

The Science of Dynamic Balance: "Balance" is not about achieving perfect equilibrium across all life domains at every moment, but rather about maintaining dynamic adjustment that honors different needs across time. *People who demonstrate the highest levels of psychological wellbeing don't divide their attention equally among all areas, but rather engage in "rhythmic cycling" - giving focused attention to different domains in appropriate seasons while maintaining awareness of all areas.*

A comprehensive analysis of work-life balance found that the most satisfied individuals develop "integration strategies" rather than "separation strategies". Instead of trying to keep different life areas completely separate, they find ways for their values, growth, and energy to flow between domains in mutually supportive ways.

The Neuroscience of Attention Management: Brain imaging has supported the previous finding that constantly switching attention between multiple competing priorities overwhelms "cognitive load" and depletes mental resources and reduces effectiveness across all domains. However, completely ignoring important life areas creates stress responses that ultimately interfere with performance in the areas receiving attention

The solution appears to lie in "attention rhythms" - deliberately cycling focused attention between different life domains while maintaining background awareness of others. This might involve seasonal rhythms (focusing more intensively on health during certain months, career development during others), weekly rhythms (dedicating specific days to different priorities), or daily rhythms (giving primary attention to work during certain hours, relationships during others).

Research-Backed Strategies for Sustainable Balance:

Domain Mapping: Clearly identifying key life domains and the relationships between them supports better decision-making about time and energy allocation.

Boundary Management: Establishing clear boundaries between life domains - while maintaining permeable connections - results in higher satisfaction and lower stress.

Energy Matching: Aligning energy-intensive activities with natural energy rhythms (doing creative work during peak hours, administrative tasks during lower-energy periods) improves both effectiveness and sustainability.

Transition Rituals: Developing specific practices for moving between life domains (brief meditation when leaving work, gratitude practice before family time) maintains better presence and engagement in each area.

The Six Dimensions of Health & Wellness: A Framework for Integrated Growth

Through research and study during my master's degree and now my doctorate in social psychology, The Six Dimensions of Health & Wellness framework has been developed to provide a scientifically grounded approach to holistic development, experience, and life satisfaction. These six dimensions - emotional, mental, physical, vocational, social, and financial - are interconnected, with growth in one area supporting development in others.

The Research Foundation: This framework has consistently revealed that people who intentionally address all six dimensions report higher life satisfaction, better stress management, and more sustainable personal growth compared to those who focus on only one or two areas. This occurs because the dimensions operate synergistically - progress in one area creates energy and resources that support growth in others.

Importantly, remember that the goal isn't to achieve perfect development in all dimensions simultaneously, but rather to maintain awareness of all areas while focusing growth efforts strategically. Neglecting any dimension for extended periods eventually creates problems that undermine progress in other areas. The Six Dimensions of Health & Wellness teaches progress through the dimensions individually, from emotional through financial, and to continually repeat the cycle and thus maintain a system for evaluation and improvement of each dimension of life, leaving no dimension neglected.

The following includes many principles taught through The Six Dimensions of Health & Wellness, presenting those that directly relate to our purposes and discussion throughout this book. We will not discuss the sixth dimension, Financial Wellness, here. If you want or need to address items not included here, visit DocPrattMinistries.org to find resources and coaching services available to encourage and support your needs.

Emotional Wellness: The Foundation for All Growth

Research Basis: Emotional intelligence and emotional regulation serve as foundational skills that impact performance in virtually every other life domain. People with higher emotional wellness demonstrate better decision-making, stronger relationships, improved physical health, and greater resilience in the face of challenges.

Sustainable Practices: Several evidence-based practices are effective for maintaining emotional wellness over time:

- **Emotion Recognition:** People who can accurately identify and name emotions as they occur demonstrate better emotional regulation and decision-making.
- **Stress Management:** Developing multiple stress-management strategies (physical, cognitive, social, spiritual) maintains better emotional stability over time.
- **Optimism Cultivation:** Practicing gratitude, focusing on growth possibilities, and maintaining hope during difficulties are learnable skills that significantly impact long-term emotional wellbeing.

Mental Wellness: Lifelong Learning in Action

Research Basis: Intellectual engagement - the ongoing challenge of learning, problem-solving, and creative thinking - is crucial for cognitive health, life satisfaction, and adaptive capacity throughout life.

Sustainable Practices:

- **Curiosity Cultivation:** Regularly explore new ideas, ask questions, and seek to understand different perspectives to maintain cognitive flexibility and life engagement.
- **Skill Development:** Learning new skills - particularly those that combine cognitive, physical, and social elements - provides comprehensive cognitive benefits.
- **Creative Expression:** Engaging in creative activities supports cognitive health and provides outlets for processing life experiences.

Physical Wellness: The Energy Foundation

Research Basis: Physical health impacts cognitive function, emotional regulation, and social engagement in profound ways. Maintaining physical wellness provides better stress resilience, improved mood stability, increased cognitive clarity, and higher energy for pursuing other goals.

Sustainable Practices: Key components of sustainable physical wellness are:

- **Movement Integration**: Integrating physical activity throughout the daily routine has proven to be better than relying on scheduled exercise sessions alone.
- **Nutrition as Fuel**: Viewing food as fuel for life goals rather than restriction or indulgence leads to more sustainable eating patterns. Focusing on complete nutrition, eating in the proper order and at the proper time, and avoiding unhealthy choices has positive affect on all dimensions.
- **Rest and Recovery**: Prioritizing sleep and recovery is essential for long-term physical wellness and overall life performance.

Vocational Wellness: Purpose-Driven Work

Research Basis: People who experience their work as meaningful and aligned with their values report higher life satisfaction, better stress management, and more sustainable motivation.

Sustainable Practices:

- **Values Alignment**: Regularly evaluating how well current work aligns with personal values and making adjustments accordingly supports long-term vocational wellness.
- **Skill Development**: Continuously developing skills and seeking appropriate challenges maintains engagement and prevents stagnation.
- **Boundary Management**: Maintaining clear delineations around work time and energy allows for a more satisfying career over time.

Social Wellness: Connection and Contribution

Research Basis: Quality relationships and community connection are among the strongest predictors of life satisfaction, health, and longevity. Social wellness impacts physical health, emotional resilience, and cognitive function in measurable ways.

Sustainable Practices:

- **Relationship Investment**: Regularly investing time and attention in close relationships maintains stronger social support over time.
- **Community Contribution**: Individuals who find ways to contribute to causes larger than themselves report higher life satisfaction and sense of purpose.
- **Social Skills Development**: Continuously developing communication, empathy, and conflict resolution skills supports long-term social wellness.

Financial Wellness: Healthy is as Healthy Does

As mentioned previously, this book is not designed to address this dimension, but it is important to know that gaining a level of 'surviving' or 'thriving' (remember chapter 2?) in the first five dimensions makes the final dimension of financial wellness simple math and the fun of dreaming what could be. 'Thriving' emotional wellness does not use money to salve heartache or the unexpected ups and downs in life. 'Thriving' social wellness protects from using money to achieve social status or gain attention from people who are not aligned with our individual goals, values, or calling.

Creating Your Sustainable Rhythm: The Chuck Wagon Approach

The metaphor of a well-stocked chuck wagon provides a framework for sustainable personal development. Just as frontier travelers needed provisions for immediate needs, tools for unexpected challenges, and seeds for future planting, sustainable personal growth requires three categories of resources: daily sustenance, adaptive tools, and generative practices.

Daily Sustenance: Habits That Fuel Ongoing Growth

Sustainable change depends on developing automatic behaviors that support your goals without requiring continuous willpower. The most effective habits are those that become so integrated into daily routine that they require minimal decision-making energy.

Keystone Habits: Certain habits can naturally trigger positive changes in other areas of life. For many people, establishing a consistent morning routine, regular physical activity, or daily reflection practice creates momentum that supports growth across multiple dimensions.

Environmental Design: Modifying your environment to support desired behaviors is more effective than relying on willpower alone. This might involve preparing healthy meals in advance, creating dedicated spaces for reflection or learning, or removing obstacles to important activities.

Implementation Intentions: Creating "if-then" plans for desired behaviors provides higher consistency than relying on general intentions. For example: "If it's 6 AM, then I will spend 15 minutes in prayer and reflection" or "If I finish dinner, then I will take a 10-minute walk."

Adaptive Tools: Resources for Navigating Challenges

Resilience Practices: Resilience psychology identifies specific tools that help individuals navigate setbacks, stress, and unexpected challenges while maintaining forward momentum. These include cognitive reframing techniques, stress management strategies, and social support systems.

Growth Mindset Tools: Developing specific practices for learning from failure, embracing challenges, and viewing obstacles are opportunities to achieve higher motivation and achievement over time.

Assessment and Adjustment: Individuals who regularly assess their progress and make strategic adjustments demonstrate more sustainable growth than those who rigidly adhere to initial plans.

Generative Practices: Seeds for Future Growth

Mentoring and Teaching: Those who find ways to share the learning and growth gained with others experience enhanced meaning, deeper understanding, and continued motivation for their own development.

Legacy Thinking: Individuals who regularly consider how their current growth serves future generations, and broader purposes maintain higher motivation during difficult periods.

Continuous Learning: Maintaining curiosity and openness to new learning throughout life brings benefits of better cognitive aging, higher life satisfaction, and more adaptive capacity.

Integration and Moving Forward: The Rhythm of a Lifetime

As we prepare to move into our final chapter on community and long-term impact, take time to recognize that the habits and rhythms you develop now will shape not just your immediate growth but your capacity for lifelong transformation and service.

The research we've explored reveals that sustainable change isn't about perfection or intense effort, but about creating systems and practices that support consistent growth over decades. The most profound transformations occur through "compound effects" - small, consistent actions that accumulate into significant change over time.

Remember that developing sustainable habits and rhythms is itself a learnable skill that improves with practice. You don't need to establish perfect systems immediately. Start with one or two key practices, allow them to become automatic, then gradually add others as your capacity grows.

Journal Prompts:

- Which of The Six Dimensions of Health & Wellness most needs attention in your current season of life?
- What daily habits could serve as "keystone practices" that naturally support growth in multiple areas?
- How might you create environmental supports for the habits you want to develop?
- What would a sustainable rhythm look like that honors both your growth goals and your current life circumstances?
- How can you regularly assess and adjust your practices to ensure they remain aligned with your authentic calling?
- What tools and resources do you need to navigate the inevitable challenges and setbacks in your growth journey?
- How might your growth and development serve others and contribute to something larger than yourself?

The journey from stuck to unstoppable isn't completed in a single season or year - it's a lifelong adventure of becoming more fully the person God created you to be. The habits and rhythms you establish now create the foundation for sustained growth, meaningful contribution, and deep satisfaction across all the decades ahead.

In our final chapter, we'll explore how your personal transformation serves not just your own flourishing but the flourishing of your community and the advancement of God's kingdom through your unique gifts and calling. But for now, rest in the assurance that every small step you take toward sustainable growth is investment in a future filled with purpose, impact, and joy.

Your life is meant to be not just a single moment of breakthrough but a sustained symphony of growth, service, and blessing that continues throughout all your days. The rhythm you establish now sets the tempo for that beautiful, ongoing composition.

Chapter 9 Summary

Key Concepts:

- Neuroplasticity enables lifelong learning and growth
- Self-awareness requires ongoing maintenance like physical fitness
- Dynamic balance across life domains, not perfect equilibrium
- The Six Dimensions work synergistically when addressed holistically

Action Items:

- Create keystone habits that support multiple dimensions
- Establish monthly self-awareness check-ins
- Design attention rhythms for different life domains
- Practice implementation intentions for habit consistency

Main Takeaway: Sustainable transformation happens through consistent, small actions repeated over time within supportive systems and rhythms.

Step #8 Power of Community

Chapter 10: The Power of Community - Building Your Support Network

"If you want to go fast, go alone. If you want to go far, go together." ~African Proverb

One of the most profound myths of our individualistic culture is that personal transformation is a solo journey - that authentic growth happens in isolation, through sheer willpower and private determination. This couldn't be further from the truth. Research across multiple disciplines consistently reveals that lasting change, meaningful growth, and sustained well-being are fundamentally relational achievements. We don't just happen to grow better in community; we are neurobiologically designed to develop through connection with others who support, challenge, and walk with us along the way.

The science is overwhelming: social support doesn't just make the journey more pleasant - it literally rewires our brains for resilience, reduces perceived stress, and creates the psychological safety necessary for authentic transformation. Strong social support networks bring better mental health outcomes, increased positive affect, and significantly reduced symptoms of anxiety and depression compared to those attempting change in isolation.

But here's what makes community support particularly powerful for personal growth: it's not just about having people around you but about having the *right* people around you. Different types of relationships serve different functions in supporting transformation, and understanding these distinctions can help you build a support network that genuinely accelerates your journey from stuck to unstoppable.

The Science of Social Support: Why We Need Community for Growth

Recent advances in neuroscience and psychology have revealed just how profoundly social connections impact our capacity for change and growth. Healthy social support operates through multiple pathways to enhance well-being and facilitate transformation.

The Stress-Buffering Effect: One of the most significant ways social support promotes growth is through the "stress-buffering effect". Perceived social support literally changes how our brains process stressful events. When we believe we have reliable support available, our stress response system functions more optimally – producing less cortisol, maintaining better cognitive function under pressure, and recovering more quickly from setbacks.

This isn't just psychological comfort - it's measurable neurobiological change. People with strong social support networks demonstrate different patterns of activation during brain scans in areas responsible for threat detection, emotional regulation, and executive functioning. Essentially, knowing you have support changes your brain's assessment of what constitutes a manageable challenge versus an overwhelming threat.

The Three Types of Social Support: Three distinct types of social support, each serving different functions in promoting growth and well-being, exhibit these benefits:

1. **Emotional Support**: This involves expressions of love, care, empathy, and concern. Emotional support creates psychological safety - the foundation necessary for vulnerability, risk-taking, and authentic self-expression. Without emotional support, people often remain defensive and closed, preventing the openness required for meaningful change.
2. **Instrumental Support**: This refers to tangible assistance, resources, and practical help. This instrumental support is particularly important during active change efforts, providing the practical resources and assistance needed to implement new behaviors and navigate challenges.
3. **Informational Support**: This includes advice, guidance, feedback, and access to knowledge. Informational support is crucial for learning and skill development, providing the external perspective and expertise that individuals often cannot access on their own.

The Relationship Between Support and Self-Efficacy: Perhaps most importantly, social support significantly enhances self-efficacy - the belief in one's ability to successfully execute behaviors necessary to produce specific performance outcomes. Receiving appropriate social support develops stronger beliefs in one's capacity to create change, which in turn predicts greater persistence, effort, and ultimate success in transformation efforts.

The Four Pillars of Transformational Support

Based on decades of research in psychology, organizational behavior, and human development, we can identify four distinct types of relationships that serve unique functions in supporting personal growth and transformation. Understanding these roles can help you intentionally cultivate a support network that addresses all aspects of your journey.

Mentors: Wisdom from the Journey Ahead

The Psychology of Mentorship: Effective mentorship operates through several key mechanisms that make it uniquely powerful for promoting growth. Mentors provide what developmental psychology calls "scaffolding" - structured support that enables individuals to achieve beyond their current independent capabilities.

Effective mentoring relationships progress through predictable stages: initiation (forming expectations and getting acquainted), cultivation (when mentors provide maximum support), separation (as mentees seek greater autonomy), and redefinition (transitioning to peer-like relationships or terminating the formal mentoring structure). Understanding these stages helps both mentors and mentees navigate the relationship with realistic expectations and appropriate boundaries.

What Makes Mentorship Effective: Several key components that distinguish effective mentoring relationships from less impactful ones are:

- **Availability and Accessibility**: Mentors who are consistently available and approachable create the psychological safety necessary for mentees to be vulnerable about their struggles and uncertainties.
- **Encouragement and Affirmation**: Effective mentors provide both challenge and support, pushing mentees toward growth while affirming their worth and potential.
- **Trust and Acceptance**: Mentees need to feel accepted for who they are currently while being encouraged toward who they can become.
- **Career and Psychosocial Support**: The most effective mentoring relationships provide both practical career guidance and emotional/psychological support.

The Developmental Network Approach: Recent observations suggest moving beyond traditional one-on-one mentoring toward "developmental networks" - multiple mentoring relationships that provide different types of support and perspective. This approach recognizes that no single mentor can meet all of an individual's developmental needs, and that having multiple mentoring relationships can provide more comprehensive support.

Finding and Maintaining Mentor Relationships:

- Look for individuals who embody the qualities and achievements you aspire to develop

- Seek mentors who have successfully navigated challenges similar to those you're facing
- Focus on character and integrity, not just competence and success
- Be prepared to receive feedback and challenge, not just encouragement
- Respect boundaries and understand that mentorship often evolves over time
- Consider both formal mentoring relationships and informal sources of wisdom and guidance

Peers: Companionship for the Journey

The Psychology of Peer Support: Relationships with individuals facing similar challenges serve unique functions that cannot be replicated by other types of support. Peer support operates on the principle of "experiential credibility" - the unique authority that comes from lived experience rather than professional training or hierarchical position.

Peer support provides several distinct benefits:

- **Reduced Isolation**: Research shows that connecting with others who face similar challenges significantly reduces feelings of isolation and normalizes the growth process.
- **Mutual Learning**: Peer relationships create opportunities for reciprocal learning, where individuals both give and receive support, enhancing the benefits for all participants.
- **Hope and Inspiration**: Seeing others successfully navigate similar challenges provides hope and concrete evidence that change is possible.

- **Authentic Understanding**: Peers can offer understanding and empathy that comes from lived experience rather than professional training.

The Neuroscience of Peer Connection: Peer relationships activate specific neural networks associated with social bonding and mutual support. Studies of community belonging show that feeling connected to peers who share similar experiences or goals literally changes brain chemistry, reducing stress hormones and increasing neurotransmitters associated with well-being and motivation.

Building Effective Peer Relationships:

- Seek peers who share similar values and growth commitments, not just similar circumstances
- Look for individuals who are genuinely committed to growth rather than just complaining about problems
- Establish clear expectations about reciprocity and mutual support
- Create regular opportunities for connection, whether through formal groups or informal relationships
- Be willing to be vulnerable about your own struggles while also celebrating others' successes
- Maintain appropriate boundaries while being genuinely supportive

Coaches: Skilled Guidance for Specific Growth

The Psychology of Coaching Relationships: Effective coaching relationships operate through several key mechanisms that distinguish them from mentoring, therapy, or peer support. Coaches provide "structured development" - systematic approaches to skill-building, goal achievement, and behavioral change.

Effective coaching relationships are built on a "working alliance" - a collaborative partnership focused on agreed-upon goals, tasks, and relational bonds. The strength of this working alliance is a significant predictor of coaching effectiveness, particularly as perceived by the person receiving coaching.

The Role of Basic Psychological Needs: Applying the established Self-Determination Theory to coaching reveals that effective coaching relationships support three fundamental psychological needs:

- **Autonomy**: Feeling volitional in organizing and regulating one's own behavior, with a sense of psychological freedom
- **Competence**: A general tendency to be interested and determined in learning new skills to better adapt to challenges
- **Relatedness**: A human predisposition toward social connection and security

Coaching relationships that support these basic psychological needs are more likely to result in sustained behavior change and goal achievement.

What Distinguishes Effective Coaches:

- **Goal-Focused Approach**: Effective coaches help clients clarify specific, achievable goals and develop systematic approaches to reaching them.

- **Skill Development**: Coaches provide structured learning opportunities and feedback to help clients develop specific capabilities.
- **Accountability Systems**: Coaches provide external accountability that helps clients maintain consistency and momentum.
- **Objective Perspective**: Coaches can offer perspective and feedback that clients cannot access independently.

When to Seek Coaching:

- When you have specific skills you want to develop or goals you want to achieve
- When you need external accountability to maintain consistency
- When you want structured approaches to personal or professional development
- When you're facing specific challenges that require targeted strategies
- When you want to accelerate progress in particular areas of growth

Cheerleaders: Encouragement for the Long Journey

The Psychology of Encouragement: While the term "cheerleader" might seem trivial in the context of serious personal development, enthusiastic, consistent encouragement plays a crucial role in sustaining motivation and resilience throughout long-term change efforts.

Cheerleading provides several psychological benefits that translate to general encouragement and support:

- **Enhanced Self-Esteem**: Receiving consistent encouragement and recognition significantly improves self-worth and confidence.
- **Improved Mental Health**: Enthusiastic support and encouragement can reduce symptoms of anxiety, depression, and interpersonal difficulties.
- **Increased Resilience**: Simply knowing you have people who believe in you and celebrate your progress enhances your ability to persist through challenges.

The Neuroscience of Positive Support: "Capitalization responses" - how people respond to others' positive events - that offers enthusiastic, supportive responses to good news actually strengthen relationships and enhance well-being for both parties. Brain imaging testing shows that receiving genuine enthusiasm and encouragement activates reward centers and reduces stress responses.

The Characteristics of Effective Cheerleaders:

- **Genuine Enthusiasm**: Perhaps it's surprising, but authentic excitement and support are more effective than forced or obligatory encouragement.
- **Consistency**: Reliable, ongoing encouragement is more impactful than sporadic or event-based support.
- **Unconditional Support**: Effective cheerleaders provide encouragement regardless of outcomes, focusing on effort and progress rather than just achievements and genuinely appreciate the person you are.
- **Celebration Focus**: People who actively celebrate others' successes contribute

significantly to sustained motivation and relationship satisfaction.

Building Your Cheerleader Network:

- Look for people who genuinely celebrate others' successes without jealousy or competition
- Seek individuals who can maintain enthusiasm even during your difficult seasons
- Find people who believe in your potential even when you doubt yourself
- Reciprocate by being a cheerleader for others in their growth journeys
- Include family members, friends, and colleagues who naturally tend toward encouragement

Character Matters: Choosing Your Support Network Wisely

Not all relationships are equally beneficial for growth and transformation. The character and motivations of your support network members significantly impact the effectiveness of their support.

The Quality vs. Quantity Research: Having a few high-quality, supportive relationships is far more beneficial for mental health and personal growth than having many casual or superficial connections. People with smaller networks of high-quality relationships demonstrate better stress management, greater life satisfaction, and more successful goal achievement than those with larger networks of lower-quality relationships.

Red Flags in Support Relationships: Be aware of these several characteristics that make relationships more harmful than helpful for personal growth:

- **Conditional Support:** Relationships in which support depends on meeting others' expectations or achieving specific outcomes can actually increase stress and reduce authentic self-expression.
- **Competitive Dynamics:** Relationships characterized by comparison, jealousy, or competition undermine rather than support personal growth efforts. I'll bet that you just thought of at least one person who fits this point.
- **Negative Emotion Contagion:** People who consistently focus on problems, complaints, and negativity can actually worsen mental health outcomes for those around them.
- **Boundary Violations:** Relationships in which individuals consistently violate boundaries, ignore limits, or make excessive demands create stress that interferes with growth.

Green Flags in Support Relationships: Conversely, several characteristics make relationships genuinely supportive of growth and transformation:

- **Consistent Reliability:** Individuals who consistently follow through on commitments and maintain stable emotional presence provide the security necessary for risk-taking and growth.
- **Growth Mindset:** Supporters who believe in the possibility of change and development create environments more conducive to transformation than those with fixed mindsets.

- **Appropriate Boundaries**: Relationships with clear, respectful boundaries allow for both intimacy and autonomy, supporting healthy development.
- **Shared Values**: Relationships built on similar core values and life priorities provide more effective support for authentic growth.

Common Goals: The Power of Aligned Purpose

Social psychology findings agree with common sense that shared goals and common purpose significantly enhance the effectiveness of support relationships. Working toward similar objectives or sharing similar values provide more effective support than those with entirely different priorities and directions.

The Neuroscience of Shared Purpose: Working toward shared goals with others activates neural networks associated with cooperation, trust, and mutual support. Sharing common purposes produces increased empathy, better communication, and greater willingness to provide assistance during difficult times.

The Role of Community Belonging: Studies of community belonging reveal that feeling connected to others who share similar values, goals, or experiences significantly enhances mental health, resilience, and motivation. This sense of belonging provides several key benefits:

- **Identity Reinforcement**: Being part of a like-minded community helps individuals maintain

clarity about their values and goals, especially during challenging periods.
- **Norm Reinforcement**: Communities with shared values and goals create social norms that support desired behaviors and discourage harmful ones.
- **Resource Sharing**: Communities organized around common purposes are more likely to share resources, information, and support effectively.
- **Accountability Systems**: Shared goals create natural accountability systems that help individuals maintain consistency and momentum.

Building Community Around Common Purpose:

- Seek out groups, organizations, or communities organized around values and goals that align with your growth objectives
- Look for people who are actively working on similar challenges or pursuing similar aspirations
- Consider both formal communities (churches, professional organizations, support groups) and informal networks (friend groups, online communities, interest-based gatherings)
- Be willing to contribute to the community's shared purposes rather than just receiving support
- Recognize that communities evolve, and it's natural for your community connections to change as you grow and develop

Building and Maintaining Your Support Network

Creating a comprehensive support network that includes mentors, peers, coaches, and cheerleaders requires intentionality, patience, and ongoing attention. Several key strategies for building and maintaining effective support relationships are:

Start with Self-Awareness: People who clearly understand their own needs, goals, and communication styles are more successful at building effective support networks. Before seeking support, spend time clarifying what types of assistance would be most helpful for your specific growth journey.

Be Strategic but Authentic: The most effective support networks are built through genuine relationships rather than purely strategic networking. Focus on building authentic connections with people you genuinely respect and enjoy, while also being intentional about ensuring your network includes the different types of support you need.

Practice Reciprocity: Sustainable support relationships involve mutual benefit rather than one-way assistance. Be prepared to offer support, encouragement, and assistance to others in your network, not just receive it.

Communicate Clearly: Relationships with clear communication about expectations, boundaries, and needs are more satisfying and effective than those with unclear or assumed expectations.

Maintain Regular Contact: Support relationships also require ongoing investment and attention to remain strong and effective. Don't wait until you're in crisis to reach out to your support network.

Be Patient with Development: Meaningful support relationships take time to develop and often go through phases of adjustment and growth. Be patient with the process and don't expect immediate intimacy or perfect understanding.

Express Gratitude: Regularly expressing appreciation and gratitude strengthens support relationships and increases others' willingness to provide ongoing assistance.

Integration and Moving Forward: Your Community for the Long Journey

As we prepare to move into our final chapter on integrating all the elements of transformation, take time to honestly assess your current support network and identify areas that may need attention or development.

The research we've explored reveals that community isn't a luxury for personal growth - it's a necessity. The most successful transformations happen within the context of supportive relationships that provide encouragement, challenge, practical assistance, and shared purpose. You cannot sustain significant change in isolation, nor should you try.

Remember that building a support network is itself a skill that improves with practice. You don't need to have perfect relationships immediately, but you do need to begin intentionally investing in the types of connections that will support your long-term growth and development.

Journal Prompts:

- Which types of support (mentors, peers, coaches, cheerleaders) are currently strong in your network, and which need development?
- What character qualities are most important to you in choosing support relationships?
- How might shared goals and common purpose strengthen your existing relationships?
- What specific steps could you take to build or strengthen relationships in areas where your support network is weak?
- How are you currently contributing to others' growth and transformation? How might you become a better source of support for those in your network?
- What barriers (fear, pride, past hurts, busy schedules) might be preventing you from building the community support you need?

The journey from stuck to unstoppable is not meant to be traveled alone. God designed us for relationship, community, and mutual support. The stronger your support network, the more sustainable your transformation will be, and the greater your capacity to help others on their own journeys toward authentic growth and meaningful contribution.

In our final chapter, we'll explore how to integrate all the elements we've discovered into a coherent, sustainable approach to lifelong transformation that serves not just your own flourishing but the flourishing of your community and the advancement of God's kingdom through your unique gifts and calling.

Chapter 10 Summary

Key Concepts:

- Social support buffers stress and enhances neurobiological resilience
- Three types of support: emotional, instrumental, informational
- Four relationship types needed: mentors, peers, coaches, cheerleaders
- Quality relationships matter more than quantity
- Shared values and goals strengthen support effectiveness

Action Items:

- Assess your current support network across all four types
- Identify gaps and actively cultivate missing relationship types
- Practice being a source of support for others
- Join communities organized around shared values and goals
- Express gratitude regularly to your support network

Main Takeaway: Transformation is fundamentally relational - you need community for accountability, wisdom, and resources that enable sustained growth.

Chapter 11: From Stuck to Unstoppable - Your Life That Matters

"The future belongs to those who believe in the beauty of their dreams." ~Eleanor Roosevelt

Here you are, at what feels like an ending but is actually the most important beginning of your life. You've journeyed through the landscape of authentic transformation, equipped yourself with research-backed tools, confronted the forces that once held you captive, and discovered the profound truth that you were created for something magnificent. The question that remains isn't whether you're capable of living an unstoppable life - you've already proven that by doing the hard work of growth. The question is: What will you do with this unstoppable momentum?

As I write these words, I'm thinking about my father, Doc Pratt, who never got to see this book but whose legacy pulses through every page. He understood something profound about living that I want to leave with you: the most meaningful lives aren't measured by what we accomplish for ourselves, but by how our growth becomes a gift that blesses others and advances God's kingdom purposes in the world.

You are no longer the person who picked up this book. You've been transformed - not by perfecting yourself, but by surrendering to the beautiful, ongoing process of becoming who God created you to be. And that transformation was never meant to end with you.

The Neuroscience of Integration: How It All Comes Together

Developmental psychology has found something remarkable about how sustained personal growth creates lasting change. When we consistently work across multiple dimensions of wellness - emotional, mental, physical, vocational, social, and financial - our brains literally develop new neural pathways that support integrated functioning. This isn't just about becoming better at individual skills; it's about becoming a fundamentally more coherent, resilient, and effective person.

The Integration Effect: What makes this particularly powerful is that growth in one dimension actually strengthens your capacity for growth in others. When you develop emotional intelligence, you become better at managing stress, which improves physical health. When you clarify your values and calling, decision-making becomes easier, which reduces mental fatigue and creates space for deeper relationships. This synergistic effect means that unstoppable living isn't about perfecting each area separately - it's about creating an upward spiral where growth begets more growth.

Creating Coherence: Psychological coherence shows that people who experience alignment between their values, goals, behaviors, and identity demonstrate significantly higher life satisfaction, better stress management, and more sustained motivation than those whose lives remain fragmented. The work you've done through this book has been building this coherence step by step.

The Six Dimensions in Dynamic Integration

Let's revisit The Six Dimensions of Health & Wellness not as separate categories to manage, but as interconnected aspects of your whole life that now work together to support your unique calling and contribution.

Emotional Wellness as Your Foundation: Your developed emotional intelligence now serves as the foundation for everything else. When you can recognize, understand, and regulate your emotions, you have the inner stability necessary for taking risks, handling setbacks, and maintaining hope during difficult seasons. This emotional foundation enables you to show up authentically in relationships, make decisions from wisdom rather than fear, and persist through the challenges that meaningful work inevitably brings.

Mental Health & Habits as Your Operating System: The thought patterns and daily rhythms you've established function like an operating system that runs automatically in the background of your life. Your mind now defaults to growth-oriented thinking, and your habits create momentum toward your goals without requiring constant willpower. This mental infrastructure frees your conscious energy to focus on contribution and creativity rather than basic maintenance.

Physical Health as Your Energy Source: Your body has become a partner in your mission rather than an obstacle to overcome. When you steward your physical health well, you have the energy and stamina necessary for sustained contribution. Physical vitality isn't vanity - it's stewardship of the vessel that carries your calling.

Vocational Wellness as Your Platform: Your work - whether paid or unpaid - now serves as a platform for expressing your unique gifts and values. Rather than just earning a living, you're creating value that serves others and advances purposes you care deeply about. This alignment between calling and contribution creates the deep satisfaction that comes from meaningful work.

Social Wellness as Your Multiplier: The relationships you've cultivated provide both support for your continued growth and channels for your expanding influence. Your social connections amplify your impact far beyond what you could accomplish alone. The people who know and trust you become conduits through which your growth influences others.

Financial Wellness as Your Freedom: Money has become a tool that serves your values rather than a master that controls your choices. Financial wellness provides the freedom to make decisions based on calling rather than desperation, to be generous rather than anxious, and to invest in long-term impact rather than just immediate survival.

Your Unique Contribution: The Crop Only You Can Provide

Throughout this book, we've returned repeatedly to the metaphor of cultivating your unique "crop" - that distinctive contribution that only you can make to the world. You've cleared the weeds, removed the stones, and created conditions for this contribution to flourish. Now it's time to step fully into the harvest season of your calling.

Your unique contribution isn't just about your career or ministry role, though it may include those. It's about the specific combination of your:

- **Authentic personality and temperament** discovered through self-awareness
- **Learned skills and expertise** developed through challenges overcome
- **Life experiences and wisdom** gained through both successes and failures
- **Values and spiritual convictions** clarified through reflection and testing
- **Relational gifts and community connections** built through intentional relationship
- **Vision for how the world could be better** shaped by your unique perspective and calling

This combination exists nowhere else in the universe. No one else has your exact history, gifting, perspective, and calling. This means there are people who need exactly what you have to offer, problems that require your unique approach to solving, and kingdom purposes that depend on your faithful stewardship of your gifts.

The Integration of Calling and Growth: What makes your contribution truly powerful is that it's been forged through your own transformation journey. You don't offer theoretical solutions - you offer tested wisdom. You don't just share information - you model what's possible. Your unstoppable life becomes the platform from which your unique gifts can serve others most effectively.

The Ripple Effect of an Unstoppable Life

Research in positive psychology consistently demonstrates that personal transformation creates ripple effects that extend far beyond the individual. When you pursue authentic growth across The Six Dimensions of Health & Wellness, you don't just change your own life - you become a catalyst for transformation in your family, workplace, church, and community.

Think about the people who have influenced your own journey toward unstoppable living. Chances are, they weren't perfect people who had everything figured out. They were individuals who had done their own inner work, faced their own obstacles, and chosen to keep growing despite setbacks and challenges. Their authenticity, resilience, and commitment to growth gave you permission to believe that transformation was possible for you too.

This is the profound responsibility and incredible privilege that comes with unstoppable living: you become living proof that change is possible, that people can grow, that lives can be transformed, and that God's purposes can be fulfilled through ordinary people who refuse to stay stuck.

Your Sphere of Influence: Right now, there are people in your life - family members, friends, colleagues, neighbors - who are watching your journey. They may not say anything directly, but they're noticing the changes in how you handle stress, pursue goals, navigate relationships, and respond to setbacks. Your unstoppable life is already influencing others, whether you realize it or not.

But imagine what becomes possible when you begin living with intentional awareness of this influence. When you understand that your continued growth doesn't just serve your own flourishing but provides hope and a practical model for others who feel stuck in their own lives.

Your Next Chapter: Strategic Areas for Continued Growth

Unstoppable living isn't about reaching a destination where growth stops - it's about developing the capacity for continuous transformation throughout all seasons of life. As you move forward, consider these strategic areas for expanding your impact:

Advanced Self-Awareness

Ongoing Assessment: Just as physical fitness requires regular evaluation and adjustment, self-awareness requires ongoing maintenance. Continue using assessment tools, seeking feedback from trusted others, and regularly reflecting on your growth patterns. The person you're becoming will have new blind spots and new potential that require fresh insight.

Spiritual Direction: Consider working with a trusted coach, pastor, or mentor who can help you discern God's leading as your capacity and calling expand. The questions you're asking now are different from the ones you asked when you started this journey.

Expanded Contribution

Mentoring Others: One of the most powerful ways to continue growing is to help others on their own transformation journeys. Teaching forces you to articulate what you've learned, and mentoring keeps you connected to the ongoing work of growth. Look for opportunities to share your story, facilitate groups, or come alongside individuals who are where you once were.

Organizational Impact: Consider how your unstoppable living can influence the systems and organizations where you have involvement. Can you bring the principles of holistic development to your workplace, church, or community groups? How might your growth serve the flourishing of larger groups of people?

Legacy Building

Long-term Vision: Begin thinking beyond your immediate goals toward the lasting impact you want to make. What would you want people to say about your life's contribution? How do you want to be remembered? What legacy do you want to leave for the next generation?

Resource Stewardship: As your capacity grows, you'll have increasing resources - time, money, influence, expertise - to steward for kingdom purposes. Begin thinking strategically about how to maximize the impact of what's been entrusted to you.

The Rhythm of Lifelong Transformation

As you move forward in unstoppable living, remember that this isn't about maintaining perfect momentum but about establishing sustainable rhythms that support continuous growth across all the seasons of your life.

Seasonal Adjustment: Different life seasons will require different focuses within The Six Dimensions. Parenting years might emphasize relational and physical wellness. Career building might highlight vocational and financial development. Later years might focus more on legacy and spiritual depth. The key is maintaining attention to all dimensions while adjusting intensity based on current needs and opportunities.

Resilience Building: Continue developing your capacity to navigate setbacks, failures, and unexpected challenges. Your unstoppable life isn't about avoiding difficulties but about having the tools, community, and inner resources to work through them constructively.

Joy and Celebration: Don't forget to celebrate the progress you've made and the growth you continue to experience. Regularly acknowledging progress achieved will provide higher motivation and life satisfaction than those who only focus on what's still lacking. Take the time to polish your trophy, throw a party, and appreciate the work you did to accomplish the goal!

Living Your Life That Matters

The title of this book promises a journey from stuck to unstoppable, but the real destination has always been a life that matters - a life that makes a difference not just in your own experience but in the lives of others and in the advancement of God's purposes in the world.

A life that matters isn't necessarily a life that's famous or wealthy or impressive by cultural standards. It's a life where your authentic gifts are fully engaged in service to something larger than yourself. It's a life where your growth becomes a gift to others. It's a life where the unique contribution that only you can make is faithfully stewarded for maximum kingdom impact.

You've done the hard work of transformation. You've developed the tools and established the foundation. You've proven that change is possible, and growth is sustainable. Now it's time to live into the fullness of what that transformation makes possible - not just for you, but for everyone whose lives you touch.

Your Continued Journey

As we conclude this book, remember that every ending is also a beginning. You're not graduating from the need for growth - you're stepping into a more mature and impactful phase of it. The principles and practices you've learned will continue to serve you, but they'll also continue to evolve as you do.

Stay connected to community. Keep learning. Continue growing. Maintain the habits and rhythms that have served you well but remain open to new approaches as your life circumstances and calling develop.

Most importantly, never forget that your transformation - the journey from stuck to unstoppable to deeply significant - is both a gift from God and a gift to the world. The person you've become through this process is exactly who the world needs you to be right now. And the person you're still becoming is part of God's ongoing plan to bring hope, healing, and flourishing to a world that desperately needs what only you can provide.

The journey continues. The best is yet to come. Step forward with confidence, knowing that you are equipped, called, and empowered for a life that matters - not just for time, but for eternity.

Welcome to your unstoppable life that matters.

Journal Prompts:

- How do you see the different dimensions of wellness working together in your life now compared to when you started this journey?
- What evidence do you see that your personal transformation is already influencing others?
- What unique contribution do you sense God calling you to make in your current season of life?
- What would it look like to live with intentional awareness of your ripple effect on others?
- How can you build rhythms and practices that support lifelong growth and contribution?
- What legacy do you want to create through your unstoppable life?

Chapter 11 Summary

🗒 Key Concepts:
- Neuroplasticity enables lifelong transformation and integration
- The Six Dimensions work synergistically when developed together
- Your unique contribution emerges from your integrated growth journey
- Personal transformation creates ripple effects that serve others
- Unstoppable living is about sustainable rhythms, not perfect momentum

⚡ Action Items:
- Develop a vision for your unique contribution and legacy
- Identify opportunities to mentor others in their growth journeys
- Create systems for ongoing self-awareness and assessment
- Design rhythms that support lifelong growth and service
- Connect your personal development to larger purposes and impact

🎯 **Main Takeaway:** Your transformation from stuck to unstoppable was always meant to serve something larger than yourself - a life that matters deeply and makes a lasting difference in the world.

Resources for Continued Growth:
For ongoing support, coaching services, advanced applications, and community connection in your journey toward unstoppable living, visit <u>DocPrattMinistries.org</u> where transformation continues at every level.

Subscribe to the newsletter to be among the first to know of upcoming books and events!

Appendices

Appendix A: Values Master List

- Acceptance
- Accomplishment
- Accountability
- Accuracy
- Achievement
- Adaptability
- Adventure
- Ambition
- Appreciation
- Authenticity
- Balance
- Beauty
- Boldness
- Calm
- Caring
- Challenge
- Charity
- Clarity
- Collaboration
- Commitment
- Community
- Compassion
- Competence
- Confidence
- Connection
- Consistency
- Contentment
- Contribution
- Cooperation
- Courage
- Courtesy
- Creativity
- Curiosity
- Dedication
- Dependability
- Determination
- Dignity
- Discipline
- Discovery
- Drive
- Education
- Effectiveness
- Efficiency
- Empathy
- Empowerment
- Encouragement
- Endurance
- Enthusiasm
- Equality
- Ethical/Integrity
- Excellence
- Fairness
- Faith
- Family
- Flexibility
- Forgiveness
- Freedom
- Friendship
- Fun
- Generosity
- Giving
- Grace
- Gratitude
- Growth
- Hard Work
- Harmony

- Health
- Honesty
- Honor
- Hope
- Humility
- Humor
- Imagination
- Inclusion
- Independence
- Influence
- Initiative
- Innovation
- Insight

- Inspiration
- Intelligence
- Joy
- Justice
- Kindness
- Knowledge
- Leadership
- Learning
- Love
- Loyalty
- Mindfulness
- Openness
- Optimism

- Order
- Passion
- Patience
- Peace
- Perseverance
- Potential
- Practicality
- Purpose
- Reliability
- Respect
- Responsibility
- Security

Appendix B: References

Chapter 1: A Round Tuit

Socrates. (399 BC). *Apology*.

Maxwell, J. C. (2007). *The 21 irrefutable laws of leadership: Follow them and people will follow you (10th anniversary ed.)*. Thomas Nelson.

Chapter 2: Stages of Growth

Erikson, E. H. (1950). *Childhood and society*. W.W. Norton.

Hettler, B. (1980). Wellness promotion on a university campus. *Family & Community Health*, 3(1), 77–95.

Maslow, A. H. (1943). A theory of human motivation. *Psychological Review*, 50(4), 370–396.

New International Version Bible. (1978). Zondervan.

Chapter 3: Step 1 Begin Within

Goleman, D. (1995). *Emotional intelligence: Why it can matter more than IQ*. Bantam Books.

Deci, E. L., & Ryan, R. M. (1985). *Intrinsic motivation and self-determination in human behavior*. Plenum.

Dweck, C. S. (2006). *Mindset: The new psychology of success*. Random House.

Duckworth, A. L. (2016). *Grit: The power of passion and perseverance*. Scribner.

Seligman, M. E. P. (1975). *Helplessness: On depression, development, and death*. W. H. Freeman.

New International Version Bible. (1978). Zondervan.

Chapter 4: Step 2 Solid Footing

Locke, E. A., & Latham, G. P. (2002). Building a practically useful theory of goal setting and task motivation. *American Psychologist*, 57(9), 705–717.

Deci, E. L., & Ryan, R. M. (1985). *Intrinsic motivation and self-determination in human behavior*. Plenum.

Dweck, C. S. (2006). *Mindset: The new psychology of success*. Random House.

Duckworth, A. L. (2016). *Grit: The power of passion and perseverance*. Scribner.

New International Version Bible. (1978). Zondervan.

Aristotle. (n.d.). *Nicomachean Ethics*.

Chapter 5: Step 3 Hindrances

Jung, C. G. (1953). *Collected Works of C.G. Jung, Volume 11: Psychology and religion*. Princeton University Press.

Kahneman, D. (2011). *Thinking, fast and slow*. Farrar, Straus and Giroux.

Rogers, C. R. (1961). *On becoming a person: A therapist's view of psychotherapy.* Houghton Mifflin.

New International Version Bible. (1978). Zondervan.

Chapter 6: Step 4 Distractions

van der Kolk, B. (2014). *The body keeps the score: Brain, mind, and body in the healing of trauma.* Viking.

Eyal, N. (2019). *Indistractable: How to control your attention and choose your life.* BenBella Books.

Chapter 7: Step 5 Weeds

DeRidder, R., & Tripathi, R. C. (Eds.). (1992). Norm violation and intergroup relations. Clarendon Press/Oxford University Press.

Tajfel, H., & Turner, J. C. (2004). The social identity theory of intergroup behavior. In J. T. Jost & J. Sidanius (Eds.), *Political psychology: Key readings* (pp. 276–293). Psychology Press.

van der Kolk, B. (2014). *The body keeps the score: Brain, mind, and body in the healing of trauma.* Viking.

Bowlby, J. (1988). *A secure base: Parent-child attachment and healthy human development.* Basic Books.

Delony, J. (n.d.). [Public talk on the "Five-Person Limit"].

Cloud, H., & Townsend, J. (1992). *Boundaries.* Zondervan.

Patrick, C., & Patrick, J. (2021). *Emotional abuse recovery.* Independently published.

Chapter 8: Step 6 Stones That Trip Us Up

Seligman, M. E. P. (2011). *Flourish: A visionary new understanding of happiness and well-being.* Free Press.

Dweck, C. S. (2006). *Mindset: The new psychology of success.* Random House.

Ryan, R. M., & Deci, E. L. (2000). Self-determination theory and the facilitation of intrinsic motivation, social development, and well-being. *American Psychologist,* 55(1), 68–78.

Research on resilience: Bonanno, G. A. (2004). Loss, trauma, and human resilience. *American Psychologist,* 59(1), 20–28.

Achievement motivation and "glory days": Vallerand, R. J., & Losier, G. F. (1999). An integrative analysis of intrinsic and extrinsic motivation in sport. *Journal of Applied Sport Psychology,* 11(1), 142–169.

Chapter 9: Step 7 Habits Rhythms

Aristotle. (n.d.). *Nicomachean Ethics.*

Doidge, N. (2007). *The brain that changes itself.* Viking.

De Meuse, K. P., Dai, G., & Hallenbeck, G. S. (2010). Learning agility: A construct whose time has come. *Consulting Psychology Journal: Practice and Research*, 62(2), 119–130.

New International Version Bible. (1978). Zondervan.

Chapter 10: Step 8 Power of Community

Cohen, S., & Wills, T. A. (1985). Stress, social support, and the buffering hypothesis. *Psychological Bulletin*, 98(2), 310–357.

Bandura, A. (1997). *Self-efficacy: The exercise of control*. Freeman.

Crisp, G., & Cruz, I. (2009). Mentoring college students: A critical review of the literature between 1990 and 2007. *Research in Higher Education*, 50, 525–545.

Uchino, B. N. (2009). Understanding the links between social support and physical health. *Perspectives on Psychological Science*, 4(3), 236–255.

New International Version Bible. (1978). Zondervan.

Chapter 11: From Stuck to Unstoppable – Your Life That Matters

James, W. (1890). *The principles of psychology*. Henry Holt and Company.

Roosevelt, E. (for quoted inspiration; verify source for complete citation).

New International Version Bible. (1978). Zondervan.

Appendix C: The 8 Steps

1. **Begin Within**
   Embrace self-awareness and honesty. Assess where you are, who you are, and define your core values and identity.
2. **Solid Footing**
   Build on a firm foundation. Clarify your core beliefs, set motivating goals, and establish routines that support your purpose.
3. **Hindrances**
   Identify and overcome obstacles. Recognize internal and external barriers - including mindsets, habits, and limiting beliefs - that keep you stagnant.
4. **Distractions**
   Manage and eliminate distractions. Cultivate focus by removing what pulls your attention away from your goals and well-being.
5. **Weeds**
   Address negative influences and relationships. Set healthy boundaries and surround yourself with supportive, growth-oriented people.
6. **Stones That Trip Us Up**
   Heal from harm and setbacks. Process hurts, practice resilience, and turn failures into opportunities for wisdom and growth.
7. **Habits & Rhythms**
   Establish positive routines. Develop habits and life rhythms that reinforce your progress, well-being, and continued development.
8. **Power of Community**
   Flourish through connection. Engage with a supportive community for accountability, encouragement, and shared purpose on your growth journey.

Appendix D: The Six Dimensions of Health & Wellness

The Six Dimensions of Health & Wellness framework, written by Amy C. Pratt as a foundational curriculum for Doc Pratt Ministries, offers a holistic, neurobiologically informed approach to personal growth and flourishing, integrating emotional, mental, physical, vocational, social, and financial wellness to support transformation and lifelong adaptation.

1. **Emotional Wellness**
   Explore identity, understand emotions, and engage spiritual wellness to cultivate self-awareness, emotional regulation, and a sense of purpose.
2. **Mental Health & Habits**
   Develop supportive routines and cognitive habits to promote resilience, lifelong learning, and intentional growth within a nurturing community.
3. **Physical Health**
   Prioritize nutrition, exercise, and medical self-care based on up-to-date research to sustain energy, well-being, and overall health.
4. **Vocational Wellness**
   Align strengths, skills, and passions in career and personal calling, reflecting on seasons of life and planning for meaningful transitions.
5. **Social Wellness**
   Foster healthy relationships, strong communication, and appropriate boundaries to nurture belonging, support, and social growth.

6. **Financial Wellness**
    Embrace wise planning and personalized financial strategies to visualize goals, manage resources, and secure long-term stability for all seasons of life.

This integrated model guides ongoing self-assessment, supports balanced decision-making, and encourages sustainable progress toward clear, fulfilling personal goals.

For more information, visit docprattministries.org/six-dimensions.

Appendix E: Doc Pratt Ministries' Origin and Mission

Doc Pratt Ministries is a faith-based, educational 501(c)(3) nonprofit dedicated to building a like-minded community "Pursuing Excellence through continual, incremental, intentional improvement in all of The Six Dimensions of Health & Wellness." Rooted in the legacy of "Doc" Pratt - a beloved physician, mentor, and community leader - our ministry seeks to honor his example of integrity, wisdom, and servant leadership by empowering individuals and communities to thrive in every area of life.

Who Was Doc Pratt?

If you had the privilege of knowing Doc Pratt, you remember his towering presence (6'6"!), his tireless work ethic, and his unwavering kindness. For decades, he served his community as an internal medicine physician, Sunday School teacher, and friend, always encouraging others to celebrate life and pursue their best selves.

His legacy lives on through his family, countless patients, and now, through Doc Pratt Ministries.

Neurobiologically-Based

Neurobiology reveals our brain's right hemisphere, which governs relationships and emotional processing, is actually the driver of lasting character change and personal growth - not the left hemisphere's rational knowledge and willpower. A "full-brained" approach that integrates both relational and rational approaches is necessary for authentic and lasting transformation.

Doc Pratt Ministries addresses this neurobiological reality through our comprehensive social psychology approach.

What We Do

Doc Pratt Ministries offers a holistic approach to personal growth through our original curriculum, The Six Dimensions of Health & Wellness. Our programs are designed for anyone seeking personal growth, whether through individual coaching, group study, community events, or discipleship classes. Authentic transformation requires attention to the whole person and supportive relationships.

Programs & Services

Coaching & Workshops: Led by Coach Amy Pratt, our coaching services help clients define goals, build healthy habits, and achieve lasting change. Corporate seminars and workshops are also available for teams and organizations.

Community Events: Through "Doc's Place," we foster connection and service with family-style gatherings, annual retreats, and opportunities for meaningful relationships.

Berean Scholars: Our book clubs and discipleship classes encourage continual, lifelong learning, drawing on both classic, well-established resources and contemporary research.

Inspirational Content: Weekly podcasts, daily inspiration shorts, and blogs provide encouragement and practical tools for confidence and success in life and money.

Our Approach

At Doc Pratt Ministries, we believe that pursuing excellence is a lifelong journey. Our curriculum is designed to be revisited regularly, helping individuals assess their progress and adapt as life changes. We emphasize community, accountability, and servant leadership, following Doc Pratt's example of strengthening ourselves so we can inspire and serve others.

Join Us!

Whether you are seeking personal growth, looking for community, or wanting to honor Doc Pratt's legacy, we invite you to be part of Doc Pratt Ministries. Together, we pursue excellence - one intentional step at a time. Visit docprattministries.org to learn how!

For more information on how to support Doc Pratt Ministries (faith-based 501c3 nonprofit) visit docprattministries.org/support. Thank you!

www.ingramcontent.com/pod-product-compliance
Lightning Source LLC
Chambersburg PA
CBHW070731160426
43192CB00009B/1401